California
Blue-Ribbon Trout Streams

Bill Sunderland and Dale Lackey

A *Frank*
mato
PORTLAND

Published in 1998 by: Frank Amato Publications, Inc. • PO Box 82112 • Portland, Oregon 97282 • (503) 653-8108

Softbound
ISBN: 1-57188-110-7   UPC: 0-66066-00305-8

Photos: Rick E. Martin   Maps: Dale Lackey
Flies tied by Jeff Yamagata of the A-1 Fish Fly Shop, Oakland, Ca.

1 3 5 7 9 10 8 6 4 2
Printed in Hong Kong, China

Table of Contents

CALIFORNIA BLUE-RIBBON TROUT STREAMS

REVISED EDITION

Introduction

A mature bald eagle surveys its domain on the Eastern Slope of the Sierra Nevada.

California offers fine trout fishing, partly because it has such varied geography. There are goldens in High Sierra lakes, mackinaws in Lake Tahoe, and rainbows, browns, brookies and cutthroats in the myriad streams, rivers, lakes and reservoirs that are everywhere.

That's the problem—there is such a smorgasbord of good trout fishing in California that anglers often have trouble deciding where to go and how to fish an area when they get there.

Some spots are well-known: Hat Creek, McCloud River, Fall River, Upper Sacramento. But what about such jewels as Heenan Lake, Kings River, East Carson River and Pleasant Valley?

That's what this book is about, where to go and the best fishing methods to use when you get there.

There isn't enough room in one book to offer details of every trout fishing area in California—such a book would look like the Los Angeles Yellow Pages. Instead, we have chosen a variety of localities that stretch from the Owens River near Mammoth Lakes on the eastern slope of the Sierra Nevada to the Upper Sacramento River north of Lake Shasta. We believe these regions contain most of the best fishing in the state.

We have selected areas you can get to by automobile, with only an occasional spot where four-wheel-drive may be required. Some are well-known and an angler certainly will have company fishing there. Others, despite this drive-up ability, offer those who prefer to fish alone an opportunity to do so if he or she is willing to hike up or down the stream. We've noted that within easy hiking distance, several miles at the most, there may be a lake or stream you might want to try. But we have stayed away from the long hikes that often are necessary to reach some of the prime High Sierra lakes.

In addition to our first-hand knowledge of the rivers, streams and lakes, we quote the "experts"—guides, sporting goods shop owners and employees, and locals who have fished an area day in and day out, year after year. This has paid off with the best inside information, the kind of angling know-how that takes years to learn.

Each chapter covers a specific area that can be fished as a "destination package". Sometimes it is a drainage area, but in other chapters, such as the one on the Upper Sacramento, the river itself is so long and varied that it alone remains the focus.

The book is designed for use by fly fishermen and by bait and spin anglers. It tells which fly patterns are popular and what lures or bait the locals depend on. In most cases, more detail is provided for the fly fisherman since the type and size of flies needed to match local hatches can be important, while a limited variety of bait and lures are used for trout fishing. In addition, there are more and more catch-and-release and special regulation areas in California, most of them restricted to barbless hooks and artificial lures, some of them to fly-fishing-only.

Most important, we describe accurately and honestly what to expect when you fish a river, stream or lake. If there are no big fish, you'll know before driving 250 miles that 10-inch brookies are the best you can hope to catch. Or, if your prime objective is to get your limit each day, we detail sections where there are regular plants by the

Above Sims on the Upper Sacramento River.

state Department of Fish and Game and the chances are good for filling your creel.

Of course there are regulations for every stream. Where they currently are special, such as catch-and-release, fly-fishing-only, or a size and bag limit differs from the general regulations, we have noted them. But rules change, so please check the DFG's fishing regulations pamphlet, available free at most sporting goods or bait and tackle shops. It's easy to get one when buying a fishing license and then keep it with the gear you use.

We are not addressing in great detail the question of what rods, reels or lines are best. This isn't a "how-to" book but is a reference work on where to find the best trout fishing in California.

We also hope it is for the angler who truly enjoys fishing for the sake of the sport, the man or woman who plays by the rules and happily returns a wild trout to the stream or lake so it can be caught again. If you love to fish, you'll want to share the joy with those who follow you.

Catch-and-release has become a key to conservation in California. If anglers do not release wild trout then soon there will be none left. Think of fishing only for hatchery-bred trout. No more small stream brookies, only a few lunker browns, no High Sierra goldens, an occasional Lahontan cutthroat.

There is nothing wrong with taking a limit of planted rainbows; that's why the Department of Fish and Game dumps millions of them into California streams each year. In any case their chance of living into the next season is small because hatchery-bred trout do not compete well in the wild world.

But that wild brookie, brown or cutthroat caught away from easy-access areas planted with rainbows is a true prize. Life is tougher there and only the fighters survive. With rare exceptions (there's nothing like a campfire breakfast of eight-inch brook trout plentiful in the Sierra Nevada) put them back.

Using barbless hooks helps. Despite a common misconception, only occasionally is a fish lost because the hook has a pressed-down barb. For fly fishermen there's a more selfish reason—a barbless hook in the ear is a lot easier to get out and may not require a trip to the nearest emergency room.

If you are going to put a fish back, don't play it too long. Studies show that some trout caught and released die anyway because they were played to exhaustion or handled roughly while being returned to the water. Never touch a fish's gills and if possible hold them in slow water while removing the hook. Don't just toss them back in—hold them gently facing upstream, moving them slowly backward and forward to allow water to flow through their gills, until they are strong enough to swim quickly away from your hands. We hope we are trying to convert anglers who already are true believers but a bit more preaching can't hurt.

Our theory of fishing, such as it is, doesn't conform to the "bigger is better" school of thought. Catching big trout is fun but a day of flipping dry flies to eight- and 10-inch brookies can be just as exciting. And hooking a 12-inch brown from a clear mountain creek where you think there is nothing but small rainbows, particularly on a light-weight rod, is as much fun as tying into a 20-incher in a trophy trout area.

Part of the trout fishing experience is where it takes place. You don't find trout in polluted, luke-warm streams. They're shy creatures demanding the purest of water. They live in areas such as the Trinity Alps, the Sierra Nevada, or Sequoia National Forest. What a combination—bliss indeed!

Be sure and preserve both California's trout fishing and the natural beauty for your grandchildren.

Lure and Bait Fishing

By Dale Lackey

Lures

The most popular lures for trout are spinners and spoons. Spinners have a main body, usually made of metal, that often is simply a wire strung with colored beads. When retrieved, the blade spins around the body.

Heavy spinners, such as Panther Martins, are designed to be cast and retrieved. Others have a light body made of beads and paper-thin blades and can be cast and retrieved or drift-fished to roll along the bottom in moving water.

Spoons are stamped from a single piece of metal with a concave or twisted shape to make them wiggle as they are retrieved. Spoons can be trolled, or cast and retrieved. Plugs such as Rapalas imitate baitfish and are either cast and retrieved or trolled behind a boat.

When fishing a stream with a spoon or a spinner, be sure to tie a snap swivel on the end of the line to keep it from being twisted by the lure as it spins. And add enough weight to get the lure to the bottom of the stream.

In moving water, cast the lure upstream and let it sink to near the bottom. The pressure of the current against the line will carry it downstream and make the blades flash. The blades do not have to spin fast to catch fish.

The lure also can be cast across the stream. As soon as it hits the water, tighten the line and let it swing across the current in an arc. If it begins to sink in slow current, retrieve just fast enough to keep it off the bottom.

A third technique is to cast the lure upstream to the head of a deep pool, let it sink, then retrieve it quickly past the head of the pool, which is an excellent holding area for trout.

The final technique is to troll it behind a boat. Use enough weight to keep the lure under the surface and down to the level where the fish are holding. The problem obviously is to find out where the fish are, and experimenting at different depths often is the only way.

The most common mistake made by trollers is going too fast. To determine the proper speed, lower the lure just below the surface alongside the boat and adjust the boat speed until the lure resembles a fish moving through the water. A spoon should swing back and forth, and the blades of a spinner should move slowly enough that you can see them as they spin.

One other way to fish a spinner in a stream is to suspend it below a sliding bobber. Adjust the bobber depth so the spinner barely clears or lightly drags along the bottom. Spinners with very light blades are best for this. Select a spot where you feel the fish are holding and cast above it. Make sure you cast far enough upstream to allow the spinner to sink. Watch the bobber carefully for any hesitation. This works better in turbulent water than in calm pools.

Whenever you use any kind of lure, cast to a specific area, especially if you are moving through in a boat.

Several years ago while guiding for steelhead on the Klamath River, we spent most of the day casting and retrieving Panther Martins. I was hooking more than half the fish we caught although I was fishing less than 10 percent of the time. I began watching to see what I did that was different from my guests.

As the boat drifted downstream, I would cast only to likely fish holding areas. My guests used the shotgun approach, casting and retrieving, then casting again without any thought to what they were casting to. I began pointing to spots for them to cast to, and instructed them not to cast unless it was into a good looking area. The shotgun approach left them unprepared as we passed good spots, rocks and eddies, because most of the time their lines were already in the water.

As they began to conserve their casts, the number of fish they caught went way up. In fact, they were casting into the areas they had been leaving for me and I was too busy netting their fish to be able to fish myself.

Plugs

Plugs are fished much like spinners, cast and retrieved from the shoreline or an anchored boat, or by trolling.

Years ago, a class of plugs called self-diving plugs, was created for trolling without having to use weight to get the plugs under the surface. This was accomplished by adding a bill to the head of the plug which forced it under water and caused it to wiggle back and forth. Self-diving plugs, like Hot Shots, Wee Warts and Flatfish, became very effective in areas where fish were near the surface, and in situations where slow trolling was necessary. In time, river anglers found they could "back troll" these plugs by holding their boat against the current and letting the force of the water moving past the plug actually pull it under the surface and put some action on it. This became an effective technique for salmon and steelhead, and can be very effective on larger rivers for rainbows and browns. Back-trolled plugs have the effect of annoying fish holding in feeding zones or in areas that trigger their territorial instincts.

When a fish hits a back-trolled plug that has been darting back and forth in its face, it's not a casual take. The plug is slammed by a fish that is intent upon either killing it or driving it away. These are exciting strikes and can add a great deal of anticipation to a fishing trip.

Bait

Protein in its various forms is the most consistent way to catch fish—night crawlers, grasshoppers, minnows, salmon eggs, crickets, cheese and all of the various concoctions that have come on the market in recent years. Berkley Power Bait took the market by storm a few years ago. Since then other manufacturers are now marketing similar types of bait: Jake's Sierra Gold, for one.

The most common method of fishing bait is to let it soak on the bottom, or to suspend it off the bottom with a bobber. But that works only if fish are moving through an area or if they are milling around in a pool.

Most of the time, you'll do better by taking the bait to the fish.

Drift fishing is where the bait rolls along the bottom of a stream, carried by the current. About 24 inches above the hook, either tie a barrel swivel into the line and put a sliding sinker on the line above the swivel or crimp a few pieces of split shot onto the monofilament. Either way, make sure to use enough weight to get the bait to the bottom. It is necessary for the bait to sink fast but it must be light enough to allow the current to roll it along the bottom.

It is actually the pressure of the current on the line that carries the rig downstream. You will feel the weight bounce along, hitting rocks, gravel and snags. If the line hesitates for any reason, set the hook—a fish may have picked up the bait. More likely it will be the line hanging up on a snag, but setting the hook

is good insurance since you would have to pull it free anyway.

The main drawback of drift fishing is that a lot of gear is lost on the bottom. On the other hand, it is one of the most effective ways to catch big trout, and you will learn a great deal about the structure of the stream. Be sure to take plenty of tackle and bait for this type of fishing.

Many people fishing a quiet pool or lake are content to let a night crawler soak on the bottom. That works if the fish are moving. If they aren't, they'll never find the bait unless it is well placed. Try dragging the bait, especially a night crawler, along the bottom. Retrieve it very slowly a foot or so, then let it rest. Then retrieve again. Suspending a night crawler off the bottom is one of the most effective bait-fishing techniques there is. Slide a sliding sinker up the line, then tie on a swivel. Tie a short leader on the other end, from 12 inches to four feet long, with your hook on the end. Bait up with a night crawler, then use a hypodermic syringe to inject air into the worm, or use a small marshmallow with the worm, to float it up from the bottom. Before you cast, drop the bait into the water to make sure it will float. Fish swimming above the bottom are far more likely to encounter the bait than if it sits lifelessly on the bottom.

Another technique is to fish the bait under a bobber. Set the bobber so the line is a bit shorter than the water depth, thereby keeping the bait just off the bottom. If fishing a stream, cast it up and let it come down with the current. If fishing a lake, start deep and gradually set it shallower until you find the depth the fish are holding.

Hook live minnows behind the dorsal fin so they can swim around. Dead minnows are hooked through the lips. Thread a night crawler on a worm threader and slide it over the hook and up the line.

Salmon eggs or Power Bait can be pushed on the hook. Just remember to use a small enough hook so that the bait will hide almost all of it.

If you feel you've covered a pool and nothing is happening, move on. You can always come back later.

There is one common denominator among anglers who catch lots of fish—they fish every cast as though they believe it is going to catch a fish. That's every cast. When they no longer feel that way, they rest for a while then continue fishing when they feel better.

The bottom line is this: Fish every instant of every cast as though the biggest fish of your life is about to hit. When it does, you will be ready.

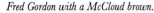
Fred Gordon with a McCloud brown.

Fly Fishing

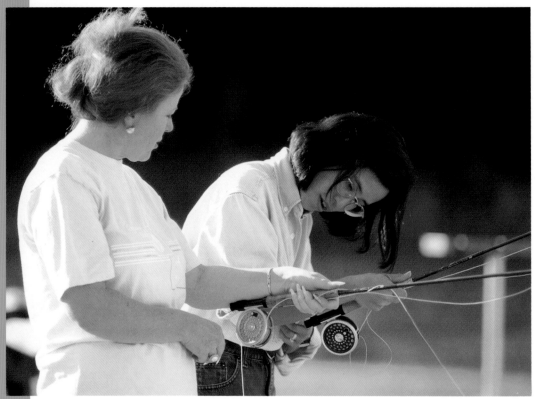

Carol Von Raesfeld with Sheri Eng giving a casting lesson.

By Bill Sunderland

There's no mystery to fly fishing; like most other sports it just takes a bit of patience and practice to get it right.

It is well worth the time. I've done most types of fishing, both saltwater and freshwater, and the sensation of working a fly on a Sierra creek is as good as it gets. There's a deep, personal satisfaction from overcoming currents, streamside shrubbery and all the other impediments to attain a drag-free float that brings a rainbow or brookie slamming to the surface after that tiny piece of fur and feathers. It is a step above what I've ever achieved with lures or bait.

If I'm preaching to the converted your time is better spent fishing. However, if you have considered trying fly fishing but never got around to it, or were unsure how to start, maybe this will help.

Women in particular are joining the fly-fishing community in increasing numbers. They are an important enough factor so that manufacturers, somewhat belatedly, recognize that they are built differently than men. Now, instead of dying a fishing vest pink and calling it a product for women, they have done such things as eliminate the chest pockets (uncomfortable on women) while adding more pockets on the side. Women's waders are built with more stretch through the hip and the crotch is seamless, which is much more comfortable.

Rods are being made with smaller handles for a woman's smaller grip—great for me, since I have a small hand and had to sand down cork grips to the size I wanted.

It's not only the equipment—there are a growing number of women-only fly fishing clubs across the nation and women are recognized as not only excellent anglers but as first-rate instructors.

Casting teachers have found that women often are more apt pupils. Men, when it doesn't go right, instinctively try to force their cast, overpower it with muscle. Women instead work at developing the rhythm, which is the true essence of fly casting.

Fly fishing, more than most other types of angling, can be an expensive hobby, what with graphite rods, milled aluminum reels, a dozen different fly lines, neoprene waders, a vest laden with 15 pounds of gadgets that may be used once in a lifetime and an entomological encyclopedia of flies that cost from $1.75 to $3 apiece and mostly end up in trees 12 feet above the water line.

"There goes $2,000 on the hoof," is the caustic comment of many a bait-slinger watching a fully outfitted fly fisherman. There's a lot of truth to that remark. The other side of the coin is simple: Buying fly-fishing gear can be fun, particularly if you are one of the lucky ones who can afford it.

Fun, but certainly not necessary.

What you do need to start with are a rod, reel and fly line. Several companies make beginner's packages that include all three for around $200. That's probably as cheap as it is going to get for serviceable equipment, less than you'll spend buying the gear separately. It is important, however, that you know what you are getting, so here is some detail on basic equipment.

Rods: A top-of-the-line graphite rod costs well over $400. Rods that are fine for a beginning fly angler are available for much less and in recent years several companies have come along that offer very good rods at half the cost of the big-name manufacturers. They also offer excellent guarantees—some a flat "we'll replace it free" if you break a rod.

Casting is the key to fly fishing and buying a really cheap rod will make learning that much more difficult because most of them cast like car antennas. Stick with graphite—fiberglass is outdated and bamboo is out of sight. If you are lucky enough to have inherited a couple of grandpa's bamboo rods, leave them in the closet until you know what you are doing. Even then, you may end up selling them to buy good graphite rods.

Rods come in different lengths and weights. The weight refers to the line it is designed to cast, with 1-weight being the lightest and 14- or 15-weight about the heaviest. Very light rods (3 and below) are hard to cast in any breeze or for any distance, and the heaviest rods (12 and up) are designed for fighting marlin, sailfish and other big saltwater species. An all-purpose rod that can be used anyplace from a creek to a good-sized river is a 5- or 6-weight.

The weight of line fly-fishing rods are designed to cast is marked on them, generally near the logo of the maker. As to length, stick to the all-purpose range of 8 1/2 or 9 feet. Using a fly rod isn't like flipping a lure with a 6-foot boat rod; you need some backbone.

Lines: You must match the line to the rod. In other words, if you buy a 6-weight rod you need a 6-weight line to go with it. There is a variety of lines on the market and you should know

some basics before deciding what to buy. First, some lines are designed to float and others are designed to sink. Sinking lines come in a number of densities that make them sink at different rates. Other lines are made to float except for the final 10 feet or so and are called sink-tip lines. To start get a cheap floating line. Since you need to practice, often on lawn or pavement when no water is available, it'll take a beating.

Even floating lines come in different types, mostly designed to help casting. A level line is just that—the entire line, usually about 70 to 80 feet, has no taper. Few of these are left, and you don't want one anyway.

Generally, lines are marked "weight forward." This is designed to make them easier to cast since it is the weight of the line that carries the fly to its destination, unlike spin casting where the line has almost no weight and the lure is the projectile carrying the line with it.

There are any number of good lines on the market. Each one claims to provide the ultimate in casting and most of them are effective. They also have a variety of confusing brand names such as Rocket Taper, Triangle Taper, etc., but all this means is that most of the weight is at the front end for casting purposes.

Until you are well-versed in handling a fly line, expensive lines aren't going to do you enough good to make the investment worthwhile. So on your first go-around buy a cheap line. By the time you graduate to the advanced class you'll have worn the line out anyway.

Once you start fly fishing regularly you'll also need a sinking line. Sinking lines are denser (so they will break the film of the water and sink) and as a result are harder to cast. In addition, retrieving a sinking line from under water for a cast is more difficult than pulling a line off the top of the water.

A good second line is a sink-tip line. The first 10 feet are dense enough to sink, the rest of the line is floating line. This won't work when you have to get really deep but it is an all-purpose line that is a part of every fly-fisherman's collection. You don't need to buy it on the first go-around but keep it in mind for someplace down the road.

The type of line is shown on the package. Most companies also include a sticker someplace in the package that can be peeled off and put on the spool of the reel. When you collect a half-dozen spools with different types of line on them it becomes crucial to know what each line is.

Here's a key to some common designations of fly fishing lines:

WF6F:	Weight forward, 6-weight, floating.
WF7F/S:	Weight forward, 7-weight, floating line with a sink tip.
WF8S:	Weight forward, 8-weight, sinking.

Reels: The old adage says that a fly reel is just a place to hang the line and doesn't need to be fancy. That's not always true—hooking into a monster fish can tear a cheap reel to pieces—but for your first set of gear it is true enough. Two points you might want to consider, however:

1. Get a reel for which you can buy extra spools. It's very handy to have that sink-tipped line all wrapped onto a spool, complete with leader and ready to go if you are on a stream and need to switch lines. Extra spools generally cost about half as much as the complete reel.

2. Buy a fly reel that you can "palm" to increase the drag. This means the edge of the spool, which is the part that turns with the line, is not protected by the body of the reel. Some reels

have a rim built into the body that protects the edge of the spool. While this decreases the possibility of damage to the spool, it means that if you get a big fish and want to put more pressure on it you can't put your palm gently against the outside edge of the revolving spool to increase the drag.

Most fishing reels have a built-in, adjustable drag but on cheaper reels it tends to be rough and hard to manipulate, and wears out easily. If you fish for big fish you will want to invest in a reel that is tough enough to do the job properly. However, they are expensive and to start you don't need to spend that kind of money.

Leader/Tippet: You can always tie a lure or a hook directly onto a monofilament line, but a fly line must have a leader and tippet. The leader is tapered to the end and a tippet is the additional couple of feet tied onto that. The size of a tippet is a key in your fishing since it is what will break and cost you a fish and/or a fly. The two factors of a leader/tippet setup are length and strength. A short leader for dry-fly fishing is 7 1/2 feet while for underwater nymph fishing leaders can be a bit shorter. When fishing in clear water for Harvard-educated lunkers sometimes a 15-foot leader is necessary to keep from spooking them.

Just remember that the longer and lighter the leader the tougher it is to cast properly since, like the fly, it has almost no weight and must be carried by the weight of the fly line.

"Turning over" the leader, or the fly line itself, is a common phrase. It means laying out the line and leader during the cast so that from an on-its-side U moving forward it unfolds into a straight, untangled line as it reaches the end of the cast and drops onto the water.

Leaders and tippets come with a designation that indicates their diameter. But with the advent of better materials the strength of a leader from different manufacturers can vary greatly.

For general purposes, here's a key:

1-pound test	8X	5-pound test	4X
1.5-pound test	7X	6-pound test	3X
2.5-pound test	6X	7.5-pound test	2X
4-pound test	5X	9-pound test	1X

Knots: Okay, Boy and Girl Scouts, now is the time to learn your knots. There are a few that you'll use regularly and the time spent practicing them at home, no matter how frustrating, will be repaid a thousand-fold in time spent fishing. Unless tying a tippet or a fly is automatic, every time you have to change one you'll face a problem. It also means that you won't be changing tippets or flies when you should be because you won't want to face that problem.

The leader is attached to the fly line with a needle knot or nail knot, which are about the same thing. They're handy to know, but not crucial if you have a reference diagram when you need it. In fact, some leader packages have a drawing of a needle/nail knot on them.

The tippet and leader go together with a blood knot, and the fly is attached to the tippet with an improved clinch knot. Most fly lines include a pamphlet that shows how to tie these knots. Once you have everything (and have passed your Scout knot-tying exam), you need to put it together. Start with at least 100 yards of 15- or 20-pound test braided backing on the reel. In addition to acting as a backup if you hook into a big one that takes out all your line, it will make reeling a lot easier.

Fly reels (except for big, expensive saltwater reels) are direct drive—you turn the crank once and the reel turns around once. If the line is attached directly to the spool, that means the wraps will be a lot smaller, which in turn means that every time you make a complete turn of the reel you take in less line. The way around that is to use about 100 to 150 yards of backing, which fills up about half of the reel, before you attach the backing to the fly line.

How you put the backing and line on the reel is determined by whether you cast and reel right- or left-handed. If you hold your rod in your right hand to cast, then you'll probably reel left-handed, although there are a number of anglers who cast right-handed and then switch the rod to the left hand and reel right-handed. Reels are designed to be reeled either way, but you have to put the line on so it is correct for you. You reel overhand, so once the backing is attached to the spool make certain you bring it onto the reel that way.

It's easier to make a mistake doing this than it would appear. To be right the first time attach the reel to the butt of your rod and reel the backing and line onto the gear holding it the same way you would while fishing.

Most fly lines have a built-in loop at the butt end. Use an improved clinch knot or any other small, secure knot to attach the backing to the line. Most fly lines are wound onto the spool on which they are sold so that the butt is on the outside, ready to be attached to the backing.

Once the backing and line are on the spool, attach a leader with a needle or nail knot and you're ready to go.

But Before You Go Fishing . . .

You need to learn how to use your rod. A couple of hours practice in an open space big enough to give you room for casting will have you handling 35 feet of line with reasonable accuracy. That's all you need to start—a majority of fly casting is within that range, no matter what your ability.

The Light Cahill imitates a variety of adult mayflies.

You might as well learn to cast properly the first time, since it is a learned ability rather than a "natural" action.

Probably the best (and most expensive) way is to take lessons. Fly-fishing shops almost always have instructors available. Joining a local fly-fishing club, if one is in your area, is excellent. Dues are low and they have casting classes sometime during the year. The only problem is that when they are giving classes might not be when you want to learn.

The alternative is teach-yourself books or videotapes. Personally, I'm a reader rather than a watcher so I prefer books. There are a number of excellent books on casting by Mel Krieger, Doug Swisher, Lefty Kreh and Joan Salvato Wulff, among others. Each offers his or her own technique and all are excellent. (There are almost as many "right" ways to cast as there are "wrong" ways.)

For watchers, there are videos by those who have written books and by a number of other well-known fly casters. There's an added advantage—rather than forking out the dough to buy a video you can generally rent them from local fly fishing or sporting goods stores.

And Finally . . .

You'll need a few flies to get started. Buy a couple of what are called attractors—flies that are "buggy" but do not imitate any specific insect. Royal Wulffs or Humpies are fine, size 12 or 14. They'll take care of you just about anywhere. If you are going to fish a specific area, you can always ask the local sporting goods store what the fish are biting on and then buy a few of the store's flies not only to increase your chances but as sort of payment for the information.

Flies are tied by hook size; the larger the number the smaller the fly. With rare exceptions they come in even numbers only— 8, 10, 12, etc. Most dry flies are in size 10 or smaller, all the way up to minuscule size 22s and 24s. Flies tied to imitate larvae or nymphs often are on slightly larger, heavier hooks and are fished underwater rather than floating on the surface.

Five words of caution that should appear on all gear by order of the Surgeon General: "WARNING: Fly fishing is addictive!"

Just watch out or pretty soon your old fishing buddies will be sneering at you and commenting to each other, "There goes $2,000 on the hoof."

Upper Sacramento River

Bill Sunderland sets the hook at lovely Mossbrae Falls on the Upper Sacramento River.

Some Notes on the Cantara Spill

The Upper Sacramento River stretching 38 miles from Lake Siskiyou to Lake Shasta is a river with two lives.

In the decades before the early 1990s it was a prime trout fishery offering a combination of wild rainbows and hatchery-bred fish. On July 14, 1991, a Southern Pacific Railroad train derailed at Cantara Loop and a tank car transporting a lethal soil fumigant toppled into the river and split open.

As the 19,000 gallons of deadly metam sodium drifted downriver it killed everything it touched—all fish, insects and plants in the 36 miles of the Upper Sacramento from Cantara Loop to Lake Shasta. Although the effect was short-lived and within days the deadly chemical had dissipated, the stream was left barren. It was estimated one million fish were killed, including 275,000 wild trout.

The outcry over the environmental disaster was enormous.

Southern Pacific agreed to pay $38 million to restore the river and to help the tourist town

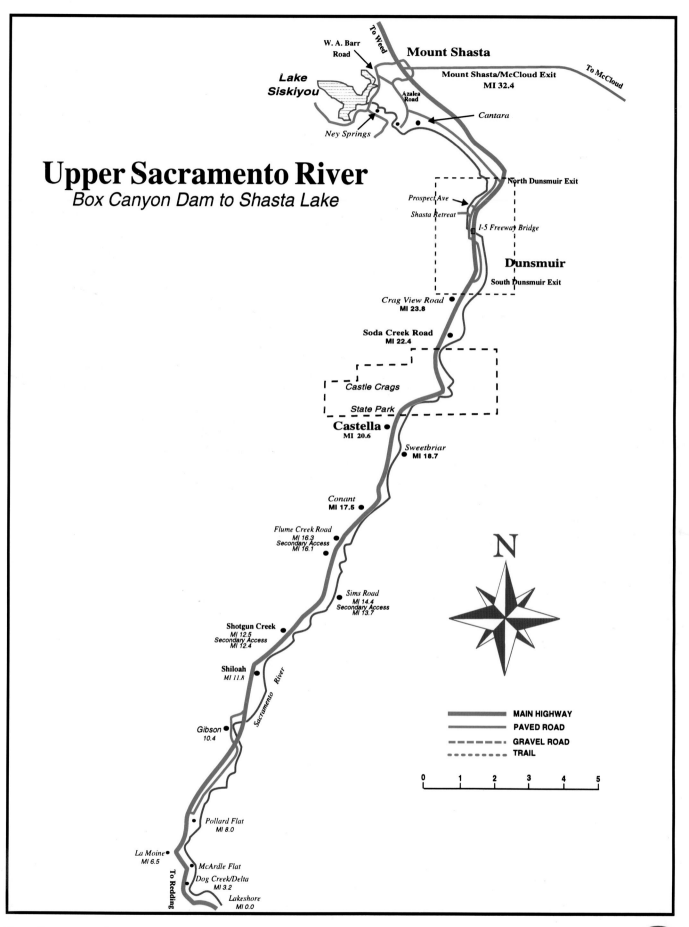

Upper Sacramento River
Box Canyon Dam to Shasta Lake

To Weed

W. A. Barr Road

Mount Shasta

Lake Siskiyou

Mount Shasta/McCloud Exit
MI 32.4

To McCloud

Azalea Road

Cantara

Ney Springs

North Dunsmuir Exit

Prospect Ave

Shasta Retreat

I-5 Freeway Bridge

Dunsmuir

South Dunsmuir Exit

Crag View Road
MI 23.8

Soda Creek Road
MI 22.4

Castle Crags

State Park

Castella
MI 20.6

Sweetbriar
MI 18.7

Conant
MI 17.5

Flume Creek Road
MI 16.3
Secondary Access
MI 16.1

Sims Road
MI 14.4
Secondary Access
MI 13.7

Shotgun Creek
MI 12.5
Secondary Access
MI 12.4

Shiloah
MI 11.8

Sacramento River

Gibson
10.4

N

Pollard Flat
MI 8.0

La Moine
MI 6.5

McArdle Flat

Dog Creek/Delta
MI 3.2

To Redding

Lakeshore
MI 0.0

MAIN HIGHWAY		
PAVED ROAD		
GRAVEL ROAD		
TRAIL		

0   1   2   3   4   5

Railroad tracks provide a convenient path for anglers along most of the 38 miles of the Upper Sacramento River.

of Dunsmuir survive the economic impact. Experts could not predict how long it would take the river to replenish itself—estimates were from a few years to at least a decade.

Then the fighting over two possible solutions began among Dunsmuir merchants and angling organizations. On one side of the battle line was a program heavily favored by Dunsmuir business owners—stock the river immediately with hatchery trout so the tourists would come to enjoy the put-and-take fishing. It was a quick fix based only on the bottom line.

The other side saw a unique opportunity to allow the river to replenish itself with wild trout and become a hallmark fishery that would draw anglers from all over the United States.

Ecologists and angling organizations, strongly supported by California Department of Fish and Game biologists, carried the day, although there were some compromises.

There were many large trout that had been upstream of the spill and in the feeder streams that had been untouched by the spill. The DFG gathered a number of these trout, bred them in hatcheries and then returned the fry to the river to live as wild trout in a major effort to speed recovery.

The regeneration of the river itself was much faster than anyone had imagined. Insects and plants grew back quickly and what trout were left alive above the spill, in feeder streams and even in Lake Shasta, took advantage of the lack of competition to feed, grow big and spawn.

Less than three years after the spill, in April 1994, the Upper Sacramento reopened.

In the end, the regulations satisfied most of the antagonists on both sides. The river became a wild trout, catch-and-release water with the exception of six miles of river beginning at Scarlett

Way Bridge in northern Dunsmuir and ending at Soda Creek south of town. This area is stocked and regulations permit anglers to keep a limit of fish.

Since the Upper Sacramento re-opened, fly-line anglers have flocked to the area and Dunsmuir seems to have thrived. There are new fly slops, first-rate restaurants and galleries.

And the fishing is great.

The Character of the Stream

The Sacramento River generally is considered to start at Big Springs, where the clear, cold water bubbles out of the ground in a spring located in the city park in the town of Mount Shasta. But the Sacramento really starts as snow on the slopes of Mount Shasta, where the melt becomes small streams that disappear underground, then reappear as myriad springs that dot the valleys surrounding the 14,162-foot-high mountain dominating Northern California.

The Upper Sacramento, from its headwaters down to the huge Shasta Lake backed up behind the dam north of Redding, is a nearly perfect trout stream, popular and productive for lure anglers as well as for fly fishers. Access along the stream is almost unlimited. The Southern Pacific Railroad tracks that follow the Sacramento through the length of the canyon offer anglers who don't mind walking the rail bed the opportunity to fish just about all of the 36 miles of stream from Cantara Loop to Shasta Lake.

Only the stream from below Lake Siskiyou to Cantara Loop can't be accessed from the tracks. But by entering the stream at Ney Springs, the angler can work his or her way upstream to the base of the dam or downstream to Cantara.

Anglers tend to congregate at the easy-to-reach spots, especially campgrounds and swimming holes. The most popular of these include Soda Creek, Sims Campground, Dog Creek and Delta. You can avoid crowds by fishing only a short walk up or downstream, even from these popular spots. Accesses are so plentiful that often a quarter-of-a-mile walk will put you into an area with total solitude.

Another feature of the river is that the geology begins changing below Sims Campground, from that of a freestone stream to areas of long pools with the characteristics of a spring creek. Anglers who have experienced spring creek fishing or would like to practice spring creek techniques, have that opportunity on the lower end of the river. On the other hand, anglers fishing the faster water on the upper river have the option of using larger, fluffier flies over fish which don't have the time to examine and pass judgment on a fly that appears suddenly and passes rapidly by.

Spinning Gear

Ultra-light spinning gear is ideal for the Upper Sacramento. Load a reel with easy-to-cast line, such as Stren or Trilene, and use a six- or seven-foot light-action rod.

Lures

Remember that only single, barbless hooks are allowed on the Upper Sacramento. Small spinners work best, one-eighth or one-quarter ounce Panther Martins, Mepps or Super Dupers, in yellow or red. The experienced angler fishes a spinner just as he would bait. Rather than cast and retrieve (which also works just fine), drift the lure along the bottom of the stream, letting the blades work in the current. This gets down to where the big fish hang out. Cast to the head of a pool, or cast above large boulders and let the spinner swing past them along the edge of the holding areas, or let it follow the edge of the main current, right in the feeding lane of the fish. Work the lure along that line of bubbles at the edge of the current.

Fly Fishing

The name of one man is synonymous with Sacramento River fly fishing—Ted Fay. Fay was known for his "dropper" double fly system. He spliced a short leader about two feet up from the end of his tippet, fishing one of his dark nymphs on the end and a dry on the dropper. The dry-fly acted as an indicator for his nymph as well as catching its own share of fish.

Since Fay's death in 1983 his flies have become icons, proudly displayed in shadow boxes by their owners. Those who knew Fay realize that he would find this reverence amusing. He never took himself as seriously as those around him did. He was a fisherman, and his flies were for fishing.

Fay is gone now, but Fred Gordon, a guide living in Dunsmuir, has fished the Sacramento for the past 40 years and knows it as well as anyone fishing it today.

Gordon's philosophy of fishing follows that of Fay: "Keep a close line and keep fishing."

According to Gordon, "Most anglers get hung up by a pretty piece of water, especially pools. If you find fish, stay put. If not, move out, cover more water, and learn the stream." Gordon follows this philosophy—just try to keep up with him on a stream that is sparsely populated with fish. He makes a couple of casts to a spot, then to another, then another, then he moves up the river and works another small area.

He doesn't wait for fish to turn on in an area. They're given just a couple of chances at a fly. "The river has plenty of fish that are willing to hit, don't bother waiting for the others," he says. "Fish on up or down the river, and come back later."

Technique

Since the river reopened to fishing in 1994, three years after the catastrophic Cantara Spill, it has been managed as a wild trout, catch-and-release fishery, with the exception of a six-mile stretch of water through the town of Dunsmuir. This area is from the bridge at Shasta Retreat on Scarlett Way downstream to the bridge at Soda Creek, where anglers may keep up to five fish per day. The entire stream may be fished with artificial lures and barbless hooks only. Because there has been a great deal of debate on the regulations regarding this stream, be sure to check current regulations before fishing.

Spring

Generally, Opening Day on the Upper Sac is good, especially if the weather is cool because you don't have snowmelt causing high flows. Because the water is cold, and usually a little high, Gordon use larger nymphs, sizes 6 to 10, and several split shot to get them down to the bottom of the river. The fish are on the bottom and won't move far for a fly.

Getting the fly down has more to do with casting than with weight. You can get the fly deeper with a floating line weighted with pieces of split shot and weighted flies than with a sinking line. Gordon uses a tuck cast where you cast high, pile up a little leader under the fly line, then throw a lot of mends upstream. As long as you keep throwing the line upstream the fly will go deeper.

Gordon prefers using a ball indicator where the fly line joins the tapered leader, preferably a three-eighths-inch Corkie because it won't hinder your cast, whereas yarn may be a problem. Don't

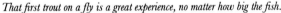
That first trout on a fly is a great experience, no matter how big the fish.

go with less than a 4X tippet that early in the season because there is more water, the fish aren't leader shy, and if you hook a nice fish, you will have a tough time getting it in because of the spring currents.

One consideration for early season fishing is that the upper river is very narrow, and during high water the upper river comes up much higher than the lower river. The lower river, which is bordered by wide gravel bars, may come up only an inch or two, offering better fishing opportunities. Another consideration is that the lower river is 1,500 feet lower in elevation, bringing warm weather earlier and generating earlier hatches of insects. The hatches actually begin in the lower river and work their way upstream.

Usually in early May, as the weather warms, however, the river becomes too high to fish because of increased snowmelt. Then Gordon fishes the Pit or the McCloud for a week or so, and waits for the river to come back down.

It is sometime between the third week in May or the first week in June that the really excellent fishing begins. During this period, there are a variety of hatches on the Upper Sac—stoneflies, caddis and mayflies. During this period there will be exciting dry-fly fishing, as well as excellent nymph fishing.

One of the most prominent hatches in April and early May is a gray-colored mayfly. Gordon uses a size 12 Parachute Adams during the hatch, which comes off around 11 a.m. and lasts until about 3 p.m. If fish aren't taking the dries, then Gordon fishes nymphs with an indicator—generally a smaller bug than he uses on Opening Day—a size 12 Prince Nymph, Bead Head Bird's Nest or Zug Bug.

For nymphing, Gordon uses a double-fly rig, one tied for fast water, another for slow water.

For fast water he slides his top fly up the tapered leader, then ties a double surgeon's knot large enough to keep the fly from sliding down past the knot. He slides another fly on about 12 inches below the first, ties another double surgeon's knot to keep that fly from sliding down, then puts two or three split shot on the bottom leader, not more than six inches below the bottom fly. This rig is fished in really fast water and bounced right along the bottom.

For slow water he rigs the first fly on the same way, then ties the second fly on 24 inches below the top fly. He puts a split shot or two somewhere between the two flies. The slow-water rig is designed to allow the lower fly to work in the current along the bottom. For this rig, Gordon usually rigs a size 12 Prince Nymph (his favorite all-purpose fly) on the bottom, with a Bead Head Bird's Nest or Zug Bug as the top fly.

Summer

As summer approaches, the hatches come off later and later until they get pushed further and further into the evening. In July and August, the hatches occur just before dark, and there won't be much right up to that time. Don't get discouraged says Gordon, just stay on the river until you can't see anymore.

Midday, Gordon fishes the very fast, aerated water. Fish your nymphs with lighter leaders, 5X or 6X, and you'll still catch fish. You will also need to reduce your fly to a size 16 Prince Nymph or Zug Bug. Gordon is always prepared with a selection of dries, like Pink Cahills, Elk Hair Caddis and Stimulators just in case the fish are working a hatch of any of the 130 varieties of insects that inhabit the Upper Sac.

Gordon also suggests that you pick your water carefully—if you aren't picking fish up in slick water, then move to the riffles

and fast water. Another option is to fish the area below Mossbrae Falls, above Dunsmuir, where cold water springs feed the river and keep the water cold throughout the summer. Gordon begins looking at that water around mid-June because normally there will be hatches every evening in the river above Dunsmuir.

Fall

Fall is a spectacular time to fish the Sacramento River from a visual as well as a fishing point of view. The cold nights start turning the leaves of the riparian foliage to brilliant colors, transforming the Sac into one of most beautiful places in California. While the river flows are still low, the cooler days allow the hatches to come off during civilized hours, offering the best fishing of the season.

During fall on the Upper Sacramento, watch for three distinct occurrences.

The October Caddis

The orange, or October, caddis come out by the thousands in the fall and can be seen skittering across the water, hanging out in the foliage along the river, and flying about during the evening mating flights. This can be a very frustrating hatch to fish because the angler tends to key on these large flies but the fish apparently haven't. Gordon tends to stick with traditional patterns, like size 14 to 16 Bead Head Bird's Nests and Prince Nymphs for fishing wet, and dry patterns such as size 14 to 16 Cahills and Parachute Adams.

The flies leave the foliage in the evening to take flight and mate, often a mile or more from the river—sometimes they make huge spots on your windshield as you drive along Interstate 5, high above the river.

After mating, the insects will make their egg-laying flights, bouncing up and down on the river's surface, but even then, the fish just do not seem to respond to them. After mating, however, the flies retire to the foliage that borders the river.

After a few days the flies begin to weaken and fall into the stream, collecting along the edges of the river. It is not until then that the fish seem to key in on them. "This holds true from Conant all the way up to the dam," says Gordon. Gordon believes the flies may be too hard for the fish to catch until they reach that stage.

When he sees dead or dying caddis floating along the edges of the river, he wades out to midstream and casts a size 8 or 10 Stimulator or Goddard Caddis toward the edge of the river, under the overhanging foliage. The fish seem to wait in these areas for the weakened caddis to fall in.

If you happen to be lucky enough to catch the October caddis when they are emerging, fishing can be fantastic, although these moments are rare for the visiting angler. This is when the flies emerge in the middle of the stream, then skitter along the water surface toward the river's edge. This activity has earned the October caddis the nickname "motorboat caddis." This is an exciting time to be fishing as the fish just can't seem to resist these big chunks of protein as they struggle to reach shore.

Midges

Another fall occurrence is the midge hatch, which takes place in the lower river. You'll see big clusters of midges on the rocks just below the surface in shallow, fast water where fish normally wouldn't be able to hold, usually in September. These look like a little worm about half an inch long.

While these insects pupate, the fish don't have access to them,

Jace Deese casts a line (and keeps the mosquitoes away with a cigar) at Cantara Loop on the Upper Sacramento River.

unless they happen to get knocked loose from the rocks by errant anglers. As these insects break loose or become adults, they drift into the pools, and the fish wait for them in the shallow water at the tailouts. This is a fun hatch to fish, but can be very difficult. For anglers accustomed to spring creek fishing, it can be great. Gordon uses a Griffith's Gnat, size 18 for this hatch.

Another technique Gordon uses is to tie a trailer on the bend of the hook with 6X tippet. Six inches or so behind the Griffith's Gnat, he ties on a size 16 or 18 black nymph, like a black version of the San Juan Worm. The fish seem to really like this setup.

Baetis

From October until the season closes in mid-November, on wet or very cold days, a small bluish gray mayfly, the *Baetis*, or blue-wing olive, comes off around midday. Gordon fishes this hatch with a size 16 or 18 Paradun, Adams, or Parachute Adams. This hatch will last from noon until around 3 p.m. If the dries don't work, try a size 16 PT Nymph.

Access

The Upper Sacramento is nearly completely accessible to the public. From Box Canyon Dam to the headwaters of Lake Shasta, Interstate 5 follows the stream, as does the Southern Pacific Rail Road tracks. Freeway exits from I-5 are treated as primary access points for the purposes of this book. Once off the freeway almost all roads either end at or cross the tracks, which follow the river. Although the exits are spaced several miles apart, the angler who is willing to walk a few minutes will find that there is no part of the river that can't be reached.

Anglers with a second car can drop one off at one access and begin fishing from another.

The accesses will be described from the lowermost at Lakeshore going upriver to Ney Springs. The freeway mileage along Interstate 5 begins with "0.0" at Lakeshore. Miles will be the distance north of the Lakeshore Exit, which is 28 miles north of Redding. The primary exits are those with a freeway offramp or major exit.

The secondary exits are roads that can be reached from the freeway but are not marked. Most of these are unimproved roads used by the Southern Pacific Railroad for track maintenance. Most of these have gates that are not locked, but keep in mind that SP could change its mind about locking the gates at anytime, particularly if vandalism or littering become a problem.

In 1985 two campers left a campfire unattended near Delta. The result was about 1,200 burned acres of timber and brush. It goes without saying that these areas are scrutinized for campfires today and citations are issued without hesitation.

If you decide to camp along the Sacramento, please do it in one of the Forest Service or private campgrounds in the area.

0.0: Lakehead Riverview Exit. This is the first river access above Shasta Lake. Take the Lakeshore Exit at Lakehead and turn right. Turn left at the tee and follow Lakeshore 1.5 miles to the end of the pavement. A rough dirt road passes to the right of two houses and goes another 0.3 mile to the river. The road ends 0.6 mile from the end of the pavement. The river here has long, slow, deep pools with long tailouts. This is a good bait and lure area. It is best fly fished early in the season when the hatches are abundant, or late when rainbows and browns from Shasta Lake come into the river to escape warm water.

3.2: Vollmers Exit. Delta: If you are driving north on I-5 when you take the exit, turn left, then right, before the road goes under the freeway. Follow the road down the hill, you will see homes on the left and the river on the right. Park at a metal gate at mile 0.7 near the houses at Delta, then follow the trail to the river.

This area has long pools, some very deep. Either fish nymphs on long leaders under an indicator, or fish the tailouts during the hatches with dries.

This is also a good area for bait and spinner fishing.

Dog Creek: Instead of going right, turn back under the freeway, and follow it until the first left, with a sign marking the Fender's Ferry Road. Follow Fender's Ferry Road one mile to a bridge that spans the Sacramento. You can park on either side of the bridge. A deep hole just below the bridge is a popular summer swimming hole.

The river can be accessed up- or downstream by walking the tracks. It can be fished from the other side by working your way upstream. There are nice riffles above the bridge, and during late evenings, you can stand on the bridge and watch sizable trout rising for caddis.

McCardle Flat: The McCardle Flat Road is marked at the freeway exit, and you will go straight ahead at the exit instead of turning right onto Delta Road. At 1.3 miles you will come to a fork, take the right fork. At 0.2 miles, turn right between two metal posts and proceed on down a dirt road. After 200 more yards, turn right to go downstream. This road ends at 0.2 miles next to the railroad tracks. It is best to park here and walk the short distance to the river. If you turn right, or upriver, instead of left, 200 yards past the metal posts, proceed on for 0.2 miles until the road ends. Park here and walk to the river, or use the railroad tracks to work your way upstream or downstream.

This area has long, slow pools and a couple of nice riffles. The riffle coming into the river bend can be fished from the opposite bank—wade the river at the end of the pool above the bend. An old rock retaining wall in the river is good for bait and lure fishermen and for dry flies at dusk. The tailout is good for evening dries. By crossing the river you can fish upstream along the opposite bank for a short ways before it becomes steep bluffs. This area can also be accessed from La Moine by walking down the tracks.

6.5: La Moine. This is a left-hand exit heading north. After the exit take the first road to the left, then stay to the right for 0.3 mile to the end of the road under the I-5 bridge. A 4X4 road takes you a short way to the end of the road next to the tracks. A staircase of riffles can be fished from the other side of the river. Wading here would be tough. By walking a dirt road on the left side of Slate Creek you can follow the river a short distance upstream to a series of long riffles.

Below La Moine the river flattens out into a chain of long pools all the way to Shasta Lake. Lots of trout are taken in this area because they come out of the lake to spawn or to avoid warm water in the lake, especially late in the season.

Be selective in this lower area—don't expect fish to be everywhere as on the upper river. Fish the riffles with nymphs and watch the pools for rising fish. Rather than fishing the pools, walk around them to the next riffle. If you don't see fish rising, move on and come back later. Don't sit on a pool waiting for it to turn on.

8.0: Pollard Flat. Although there is no river access at Pollard Flat, this exit puts you on a side road that parallels the river. About miles 1.5 is the Gibson area, a long curve with a railroad siding. You can park here and work your way upstream to long, deep pools, suitable for bait-fishing and deep nymphing techniques. A walk upriver will bring you to deep pools and narrow slots, with some riffles.

10.4: Gibson. Use the Gibson Exit to access the side road mentioned above to access the Gibson fishing area.

Mile 11: Secondary Access. This road drops off to the right at the end of a guardrail, 0.6 mile north of Gibson and opposite a freeway sign facing southbound traffic that says "Shasta Dam 30, Redding 37". A miserable 4X4 road leads down the hill to the river.

A beautiful pool greets you at the end of the road. A series of riffles can be reached by walking upriver. Downriver, riffles and pools give way to long pools near Gibson. At this point the railroad tracks are across the river and may be reached by walking downstream and crossing a railroad trestle.

11.8: Secondary Access/Shiloah. A road to the right crosses the crest of a ridge then drops a short distance toward the river. Cars can park at the top, 4X4 trucks can drive the short distance to the end of the road. Follow a trail down to the tracks. Across the river is a beautiful sandy beach and a very deep pool. This is a favorite stopping place for rafters during the early spring runoff. You can walk upriver along the tracks and fish a series of rapids, or pocket water and riffles above the rapid. Walk downriver to a series of riffles and pools.

12.5: Secondary Access/Shotgun Creek. A steep, paved road drops off the right-hand side of I-5 from a wide pull-out. The road is okay for cars. Park here and walk, or follow the road upriver paralleling the tracks to Shotgun Creek.

Mile 13.7: Secondary Access. At the north end of a large cut, just before a guardrail, a road turns off to the right between several large boulders. Follow the road 0.4 mile to the bottom of the hill and park at the end of the road.

Shotgun Creek comes in just downriver. This area has good pools and riffles and is the easiest access to the area above Shotgun Creek.

14.4: Sims Road. Follow the paved road to the bottom of the hill or cross the bridge to the Sims campground. The best access is along the railroad tracks on the west side of the river. A paved road to the left ends along the tracks after mile 0.2.

This area has riffles and fast-flowing holes with pocket water and side slots. Overhanging brush and elephant ears are in abundance.

16.1: Secondary Access. A road to the right leads down the hill to the tracks. This area has excellent riffles which are good for nymphs and dries, half pocket water, half pools. At Sims the pools get longer and slower.

16.3: Flume Creek. Park at the offramp and follow the trail through blackberry bushes down the hill and across the tracks to the river. This area is easier to access from the secondary access to the south.

17.5: Conant. At Conant the river slows even more, creating pools. From Conant downriver to Flume Creek there is little change. The pools are a little deeper but the river still has a good flow of current. At the Conant Exit a road leads off to the right then forks. Take either fork, park at the end of the road and walk to the river. The tracks allow access anywhere along this side of the river. The river in this area is primarily fast riffles and pools.

18.7: Sweetbriar. Turn left, go 0.3 mile to the end of the road and park next to the tracks. Turn right, proceed 0.5 mile to where the road crosses the tracks. A sign welcomes anglers to park near the tracks and to walk in. This is a good idea since the one-lane bridge crosses the river into a summer home area where parking is nonexistent. Upstream, the river flows through banks reinforced with concrete, channelizing it and making it too deep for good wading.

Downstream, the river is typical Upper Sac, with pools interspersed with small rapids and riffles.

20.6: Castella. Take the Castella Exit. Since the road to the right leads to an area where private homes block access to the river, go left and drive 0.5 mile to a bridge that crosses the river. Turn left toward the Castle Crags picnic area, where the river can be entered. This is mostly pocket water with a sprinkling of pools. This is more diverse than the water through Dunsmuir. Castle Creek, which is not good fishing, enters the Sacramento here.

22.4: Soda Creek. Turn right after the exit and follow the paved road 0.3 mile to the river and park on either side of the bridge. Work up or down the river along the tracks or through the brush. A large, deep pool under the bridge is a favorite with bait and lure anglers, and with swimmers.

The Soda Creek Bridge is the lower boundary of the put-and-take fishery. From here down is wild trout, catch-and-release water. From here up to the Bridge at Shasta Retreat is the only part of the river where you can keep a fish.

Dunsmuir

The area through Dunsmuir is excellent nymphing water with nearly unlimited access. You can fish nearly the entire stream just by wading the river, which averages about a foot and a half deep and is loaded with boulders and pockets.

Through Dunsmuir is the only portion of the Upper Sacramento that is stocked with rainbows, and the only area where you can keep a fish.

Following are the accesses to the Sacramento in Dunsmuir. Mileage is included when they are exits from I-5.

Railroad Park: From the sewage plant below the Railroad Park Bridge to the Soda Creek Bridge is a little over a mile. This is an awkward stretch of the river full of pea gravel and few holding spots.

23.8: Crag View Drive/Railroad Park. Take the South First Street Exit. After the exit, turn left, follow the road past a mobile home park, then turn right onto South First Avenue. Follow South First to a bridge that crosses the river. Park on the west side of the bridge. The stream can be entered from the bridge. South First follows the river upstream and can be used for access anywhere that you can park your car. Do not park in driveways or yards.

Butterfly Bridge: Follow South First Street upriver to its intersection with Butterfly Avenue, turn left to the bridge. The river can be accessed at the bridge and along Butterfly Avenue.

Sacramento Bridge: Continue upstream along South First then follow a jog onto Sacramento Avenue. Follow the river upstream to the Sacramento Bridge. Access is plentiful here.

I-5 Bridge: Follow Sacramento Avenue upstream until it passes under the I-5 freeway bridge. This whole area is accessible. The railroad tracks across the river can be walked for unlimited river access. Follow Stagecoach Avenue all the way out to the intersection with Dunsmuir Avenue.

Dunsmuir City Park: The drive to Dunsmuir City Park passes between the softball park and an old steam locomotive on display. The park has very good fishing considering the amount of pressure it receives.

Shasta Retreat or Scarlett Way: This is the last Dunsmuir access. Follow Dunsmuir Avenue north to a metal arch that says "Shasta Retreat/Scarlett Way". This is the upper boundary for stocked trout and bait-fishing, but a short hike upstream takes you into an incredible native trout fishery. A few houses come right down to the water across the river, but they don't seem to affect the fishing. Begin fishing once you pass the remains of an old footbridge that has been washed out. Shasta Retreat upstream to Mossbrae Falls is considered by many to be the best stretch of water on the river.

Prospect Avenue Fishing Access: From Dunsmuir Avenue, turn at the Cedar Lodge Motel onto Prospect Avenue. Drive 0.3 miles to a small parking area at the end of the road, and next to the river.

27.9: North Dunsmuir Exit. Take this exit to access the northern end of Dunsmuir Avenue. Turn south on Dunsmuir Avenue to access Prospect Avenue, Shasta Retreat and the Dunsmuir City Park.

Mount Shasta

Cantara to Shasta Retreat: This stretch of water takes you past Mossbrae Falls. It is approximately three miles long with plenty of water for a good day's fishing. Mossbrae Falls is easy to recognize since water cascades right out of the side of the canyon. Mossbrae is a mile and a half upriver from Shasta Retreat Bridge.

32.4: Cantara Loop. Take the McCloud/Mt. Shasta Exit, then take the first right onto Azalea. Turn right and follow the road across I-5 and keep going until you cross the railroad tracks. Turn left and proceed 0.4 mile to Cantara Street, turn right. Follow Cantara 1.3 miles to the bottom of the hill and on to the river. Park where the road meets the river.

32.4: Ney Springs. This is the uppermost access to the Sacramento River. Take the first Mount Shasta Exit, immediately past the McCloud Exit, onto Mount Shasta Boulevard. Follow it to the Lamplighter Restaurant on the left and turn left onto Ream Avenue. Follow Ream to its intersection with W.A. Barr Road and turn left. Follow W.A. Barr Road about two miles, cross Box Canyon Dam and turn left onto Castle Lake Road. About 100 yards up Castle Lake Road, take the first left onto a dirt road. Follow it to the Ney Springs Fishing Access, follow that to the end of the road. Follow the trail to the river.

The Zug Bug is an effective pattern on Fall River in the evening before the Hexagenia mayflies come off at dusk.

Chapter Four

Lower Sacramento River

The area near the Posse Grounds in downtown Redding is a favorite area for fly fishing on the Sacramento River.

The Lower Sacramento River has finally been discovered, and for good reason. It is considered by many to be the finest trout stream in California. Although the stream has yet to achieve the reputation accorded to Fall River, the McCloud or the Upper Sac, it holds what may be the largest trout population in California, and the average size fish, at a documented 16.2 inches long, is certainly among the largest.

The Lower Sac has its own character, however, and although it's open year-round, water releases from Shasta Dam dictate the fishing seasons as arbitrarily as the Fish and Game regs would.

First of all, the Lower Sacramento is the largest stream in the state. A tailwater stream fed by releases from Shasta Lake, the river water is cold and clear, providing a wonderful habitat for the fish that live there. Shasta Lake is a catch basin for the north state's finest trout water—the Upper Sac, McCloud, Hat Creek, Fall River and the Pit River. Just below Shasta Dam, a good portion, from 80 to 90 percent, of the water from the Trinity River basin is added to the Sacramento River as part of the Bureau of Reclamation's mandate to satisfy the agricultural and municipal thirst of the balance of California.

The Lower Sacramento actually begins at the base of Shasta Dam, although, for all practical purposes, the real fishing begins a few miles downstream in the City of Redding, just below the Anderson-Cottonwood Irrigation District diversion dam.

This area is adjacent to Redding's Civic Center Auditorium, the Turtle Bay Museum and the Redding Posse Grounds. For the convenience of boaters, there is also a launch ramp with parking. The area around the Civic Auditorium, from the Posse Grounds downstream to the Hwy. 299 bridge, is a large area that anglers can fish when the river flows are low enough for safe wading.

Drift boat and powerboat anglers and guides can launch at this point. Drift-boaters often fish their way downstream, and take out at a number of other launch ramps between Redding and the City of Anderson. It is this water that is most accessible, and most popular with fly and bait anglers alike.

Fly Fishing

Until the late 1980s the Sacramento was largely ignored as a trout stream except for a loyal group of locals who were willing to learn the intricacies of fishing the stream and were developing fishing techniques as well as fly patterns that would work on this stretch of water. One of these was Mike Mercer, a former fishing guide and for several years now the retail manager at The Fly Shop, a Redding landmark for fly anglers on pilgrimages to the streams of Northern California.

An avid fly fisher, Mercer's prime opportunity for fishing is the Lower Sacramento River. He's had ample opportunity to become familiar with the accesses, the river flows, and the nuances of the river's various hatches. Mike views the Sacramento as an excellent fishery throughout the year, but for wading anglers, the best times to fish are from fall, when the flows drop below 9,000 cfs, until spring, before they rise again.

Fishing from a boat can be good throughout the year, even

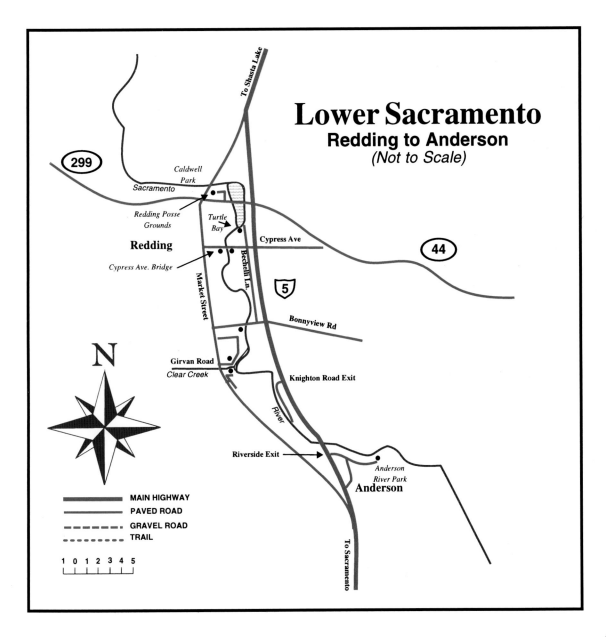

in summer when the flows rise to 15,000 cfs, although we recommend hiring a guide or fishing with an experienced boatman at these water levels.

Fall

The season for walk-in fishing actually begins in the fall, according to Mercer, around the first of October, when the flows from Shasta Dam are dropped down to 5,000 to 6,000 cfs. That almost perfectly coincides with the spawning salmon run. As the salmon begin kicking up the streambed, the trout move right in behind them to eat the bugs that are released from the river's gravel.

Mercer sees more anglers on the river—"including boat guys, the spin fishing contingent and fly anglers, all fishing Glo Bugs"— during the egg grab in October and November, when salmon are spawning in the river. You'll also see a lot of fly fishers fishing caddis behind the spawning salmon.

Mike usually doesn't fish the river until after the spawn, while salmon are still laying on the redds. "By then the Glo Bugs aren't that effective because the trout have been hammered with them," he says. Then he fishes a Z Wing Caddis which he developed, the Pulsator Caddis which incorporates a glass bead in the body, and a size 14 egg pattern developed by guide Ernie Dennison called Micro Eggs.

As the season gets closer to winter and the salmon are no longer tearing up the streambed, Mercer switches to a size 14 Gold Bead Bird's Nest. In fact, he recommends this as a year-round pattern. Although it doesn't work as well as the green caddis in the spring or mayfly nymphs in the winter, it works as well as anything else in the summer and fall.

Mercer has also learned that because of the intense pressure from anglers fishing with Glo Bugs, fishing caddis nymphs, such as the Z Wing Caddis, can be more effective than the Glo Bugs.

On any day in the fall you can see fly anglers fishing any place where they can get to the river and wade. You will first notice that almost everyone is using an indicator, usually a large piece of bright yarn, several feet above the Glo Bug or nymph.

Regarding indicators, Mercer feels that, philosophically, it would be nice if everyone could learn to fish without an indicator, to learn line control, the nuances of the current, and he says, "You feel a lot more strikes that way."

But the Lower Sac lends itself more to long line nymphing where you can't maintain line control, making the indicator a necessity. "A lot of people are amazed, though, when we fish water right in front of us that we get, or at least detect, at least two or three times as many strikes. If you're a good high-stick fisherman, you'll get a lot more strikes than an indicator fisherman." Regardless, Mercer uses an indicator a lot on the Lower Sac because it's a great way to cover a lot of water, and the long casts required on the stream make them a necessity.

Winter

During the winter months of December, January and February, the mayfly becomes the predominant insect. According to Mercer, "You've got the little *Baetis* that hatches on and off all winter, that's when we switch to small, size 16, 18 or 20 nymphs—actually spring creek patterns, fished under an indicator with a lighter tippet, usually 5X. We'll go down to 7X if we have to, but the trout on the Lower Sac really aren't leader shy. We'll use Blue-wing Olives, Sparkle Pupa, Gold Bead Bird's Nests. When we find the fish taking dries, usually once or twice a

week, we'll even use size 20 dries. But during winter, the fish are really into the smaller nymphs."

Spring

The caddis actually come a couple times a year: The spring caddis (*Brachycentrus*), when you use the Sparkle Pupa, the Z Wing Caddis, and the curved shank (LaFontaine Caddis) pupa forms. This fishing starts to come alive in March, and runs into June.

There are times, depending on the weather, when you start to see huge egg-laying flights, especially during the middle of the day. These are the caddis storms, and are so thick at times that the water is matted with the bodies of the spent adults and the water is in a constant boil as the trout harvest this incredible bounty as though it may be the last meal they ever eat. This is an incredible time to be on the river, not so much for the fishing, but to experience the pandemonium of nature at her most intense.

Summer

During summer the flows kick into full gear, running at 14,000 to 15,000 cfs, high above the ideal wading flows at 4,000 to 5,000 cfs. Forget about wading the river at this time of year, but not about fishing. This is the time to take a boat onto the river. Although the general misconception is that the river doesn't fish as well during the hot weather, the truth is the hot weather actually makes it better.

As summer approaches, an amber-bodied caddis begins to appear. Mercer says to switch to larger patterns for both nymphs and for dries, recommending size 12 to 14 Z Wings, Amber Caddis, and the Gold Bead Diving Caddis.

The best time to fish dries is during the evening hatches and the midday egg-laying flights. During the egg-laying flights, the adult caddis actually dive under water to attach their eggs to submerged rocks, then return to the surface. Consequently, they're available to the trout for a long time. Although patterns have been developed to imitate diving caddis, Mercer suggests not getting too scientific about it as most emerger patterns work pretty well. "Some guys have even found that swinging a little emerger on a tight line during the egg-laying flights, as well as during the evening emergence imitates not only the emerging caddis, but also the diving caddis very effectively."

Bait and Lure Fishing

Bait anglers have the best success on traditional baits, such as night crawlers or crickets, although some also use fresh salmon roe. The boat angler runs the boat to the upper end of a pool, casts upstream and to the side, then lets the boat drift along with the bait to create a long drift through the pool. Another method is to keep the boat next to a holding area and drift-fish the bait through the area. An observation by Hank Mautz of Professional Guide Service in Anderson, is that the bait is moving so fast along the bottom, the fish are generally hooked before they have a chance to swallow the bait as they would in quieter water, resulting in few casualties.

During the salmon spawn in fall, Glo Bugs are very effective when fished this way, Mautz has seen days where his clients have caught and released 40 to 50 fish in a day.

Glo Bugs are also effective fished from shore during the fall "salmon grab." By drift-fishing (casting and letting the current carry the bait along the bottom), the bait angler is presenting the Glo Bug to the fish in a natural manner, particularly when fished behind the spawning beds.

Lures

Back-trolling Hot Shots, Wee Warts or other diving plugs from drift boats is growing in popularity on this part of the river. Using a technique developed for steelhead fishing on the coastal streams, the oarsman holds the boat against the current while the angler runs a Hot Shot 30 to 50 feet downstream from the boat. The Hot Shot has a blade at its head that pulls the lure under the surface and makes it vibrate in the current.

The plug is worked slowly through the pool. When it enters a fish's territory it is regarded as an intruder or a smaller food fish and is attacked. Regardless of how the trout views the plug, the result is the same. Consult regulations regarding lure and hook sizes. At the time of this writing, the lure may not be over 2 1/2 inches long. Hooks may not be over 1/2 inch from point to shank, and all hooks must be barbless, from Keswick Dam to the Deschutes Road Bridge just south of the City of Anderson. This regulation is to reduce the amount of incidental hookups on salmon.

In late winter when the flows are at their lowest, spinners and spoons can be a key producer. Terry Hopper, Sacramento Valley sportsman, likes to cast Panther Martin spinners upstream, then keep a tight line as the lure drifts back in the current. "You don't have to retrieve furiously," says Hopper. "Just let the blades work in the current."

Keswick Lake

Keswick Lake, the impoundment immediately below Shasta Dam, has a lot of potential that is currently not being developed says Mercer. This is a lake version of the river with the same fish and virtually the same hatches. Although Keswick is not as easy to fish as the river because it is a lake, it has its seasons of caddis and mayflies as well as midge and *Callibaetis* hatches in the spring.

The easiest way to fish this lake is to use sinking lines with a leech pattern cast to the edge of the weed beds where the bottom drops off into the deep water, then strip in.

Access

Boat Launch Ramps

The most effective way to fish the Lower Sacramento River is by boat. Although the river is the largest in California, its fast, free-flowing character creates shallow tailouts and rapids.

The long, fast-flowing pools with shallow riffles make jet boats the most suitable craft.

Propeller-powered boats may be able to maneuver along the river during the summer when flows are high, but it's only a matter of time before someone finds a rock in mid-riffle that sticks up a little higher than the operator thought. And the Sacramento is no place to be without power.

Drift boats, the type used in the Northwest for steelhead fishing, are becoming popular because they can float over shallow areas and are very maneuverable. The only drawback is that they can go only downriver. A vehicle must be left at a downriver takeout location or the anglers may find themselves faced with a long walk back to their starting point.

Public launch ramps are at the following locations:

Caldwell Park in Redding

This is located at Lake Redding Park, where North Market Street crosses the Sacramento River. This area requires motor boats that can go upstream because the Anderson Cottonwood Irrigation District dam is located a few hundred yards down from the launch ramp.

Redding Posse Grounds

Take Highway 299 West from Interstate 5, take the Park Marina off-ramp. Turn right onto Auditorium Way, follow the road to the right and drive past the Redding Civic Auditorium to a parking lot near the horse stables. The launch ramp is at the upriver end of the parking lot.

This ramp is located on one of the best pools in the river. Anglers drift bait or back-troll plugs down either side of the river, or sweep the tailout located mid-river near some old pilings.

This area has a large population of rainbows. This is also the most heavily fished trout water on the Lower Sacramento.

There are more excellent riffles in the eight miles between

Redding and Anderson than a good angler can fish in a day. Most of the water is good riffle water for fly fishing, or pools for back-trolling.

Bonnyview Road

About four miles south of the Cypress Street Exit on Interstate 5, take the South Bonnyview Exit and turn west. About half a mile west you will cross the Sacramento River, another quarter mile, you will see a sign on the left marking the City of Redding Bonnyview Launch Ramp.

This area is excellent for launching or pulling out, but wading is dangerous.

Sacramento River RV Park

8900 Riverland Drive
Redding, CA 96002
(530) 365-6402

This is a private launch facility where a fee is charged and access could be denied at any time.

Eight miles south of Redding on Interstate 5, take the Knighton Road Exit toward the river and turn left onto Riverland Drive. Two miles later, at the end of the road, you will pass through a white arch marking the boundary of the Sacramento River RV Park. Stop at the office to register and pay a day-use fee. If no one is in the office, you can self-register. Follow the road as it winds to the left, across a dry wash, and on to the paved launch ramp and dock area.

Hank Mautz displays a full-bodied Sacramento River rainbow.

Anderson River Park

Take the Riverside Exit from I-5 and turn east. When Riverside dead ends into North Street, turn right. Turn left onto Stingy Lane, then follow Stingy Lane to where a small blue sign at the corner of Stingy and Rupert marks the entrance to Anderson River Park.

This area has a paved launch ramp, parking and restrooms.

Walk-In Access

The Posse Grounds and Turtle Bay
(See directions above)

East Turtle Bay Regional Park

Take the Cypress Exit from I-5, and turn west. At the first light, turn right onto Bechelli Lane. Follow Bechelli for about two miles to where it turns and drops sharply off the hill to a flat area near the river. This is just across the river from Turtle Bay.

Park in the gravel parking area and follow the trail to the river. This area is very popular with fly anglers.

Elk Hair Caddis. At times during the spring mating flights, the spent caddis form a mat of dead insects on the river's surface.

East End of the Cypress Street Bridge

Turn left onto Hartnell from Cypress, take the first right past the Gasomat gas station.

About one-quarter mile down Henderson is an undeveloped dirt parking area next to the river. You can follow foot trails or work your way along the river upstream, above the Cypress Avenue Bridge, or downstream about 1/4 mile. Although this (the east side of the river) is wadeable, it appears to be more popular with lure and bait anglers.

You can also continue on Hartnell just past the Raley's store, turn right onto Parkview, go 0.1 mile, turn left onto Henderson. 0.1 mile to a guard rail and a telephone pole on the left, turn onto a gravel road to the left. Follow the road along the power lines to a parking area. You can then walk down a rocky road to the river's edge. This is a short distance below the above access.

West End of the Cypress Bridge

To access the west end of the bridge, follow Cypress across the Sacramento River to the Athens Avenue Exit. Take the exit to the right, go one block to the light. Turn right onto Locust Avenue, go one block to the Tee at Park Marina Drive. Turn right, go one half block to the area under the bridge. park in the gravel area next to the river just above the bridge. At low water levels you can wade perhaps 50 yards upstream, and one-quarter mile downstream.

Girvan Road

Take the South Bonnyview Road Exit west 1.9 miles to Highway 273. Turn left onto Highway 273. Go 1.0 to the light and turn left onto Girvan Road. Follow Girvan 0.7 miles to a small City of Redding park on the right, park here and follow a trail to the river. Cross the first side channel, cross a gravel island to the next side channel. Most people fish the second side channel. Mercer says fish are in here all the time, especially when the salmon are running.

Clear Creek Road

At the intersection of South Bonnyview and Hwy. 273, turn left and drive 2.3 miles south on Hwy. 3 to River Ranch Road, turn left, cross the tracks and turn left again.

Go 2.3 miles from S. Bonnyview south to River Ranch Road. Turn left on River Ranch Road, cross the railroad tracks, then turn left again. Take the first right, which is 0.1 mile from where you turned left. This road is marked by a sign that says Property of City of Redding. This is the City of Redding Sewage Treatment Plant, which is located adjacent to Clear Creek and near its confluence with the Sacramento. 0.2 miles in, you will see a gate and a cyclone fence, with a gravel road immediately to the right that ends a short distance at a gravel parking area. Park here, walk 200 yards along a trail to the settling ponds. Walk straight on past the ponds another 100 yards, looking for a narrow trail through the blackberries down to Clear Creek. You can follow Clear Creek, or wade down the stream to the Sacramento River. Fishing in Clear Creek is prohibited, except during trout season.

Upstream on the Sacramento is a system of back channels with good fishing. Below Clear Creek is a big back channel full of carp and bass.

The Fly Shop
4140 Churn Creek Road
Redding, CA 96002
(530) 222-3555

Hank Mautz Professional Guide Service
3231 Davey Way
Anderson, CA 96007
(530) 365-8140

Lake Siskiyou and Lake Shasta

A favorite Lake Shasta species—a nice-sized rainbow.

Lake Siskiyou

The first time I fished the Sacramento was during college in the early 1960s. A friend and I took the road out of Mount Shasta and across the Steel Bridge at the entrance to Box Canyon. We followed the road upriver and began fishing. The weather turned nasty, started to rain and eventually began to snow. The car wouldn't start and we ended up walking back to town. I caught one fish that day, a six-inch rainbow. Hardly an auspicious beginning for such a great stream.

The road we used, as well as the part of the stream we fished, is now under the water of Lake Siskiyou. Formed behind the Box Canyon Dam built in the 1960s, it is now open to the public as a fine trout fishing lake. During the winter and spring of 1972 I would drive from my home in McCloud to fish the north shore with night crawlers. Catching a limit of five 12- to 16-inch rainbows was easy in those days.

Like a lot of lakes, Siskiyou's fishing has since deteriorated. It still boasts good fishing, but the lake is popular as a vacation area and summer visitors seem to catch the fish as fast as they are planted. The lake is slowly gaining a reputation as a smallmouth

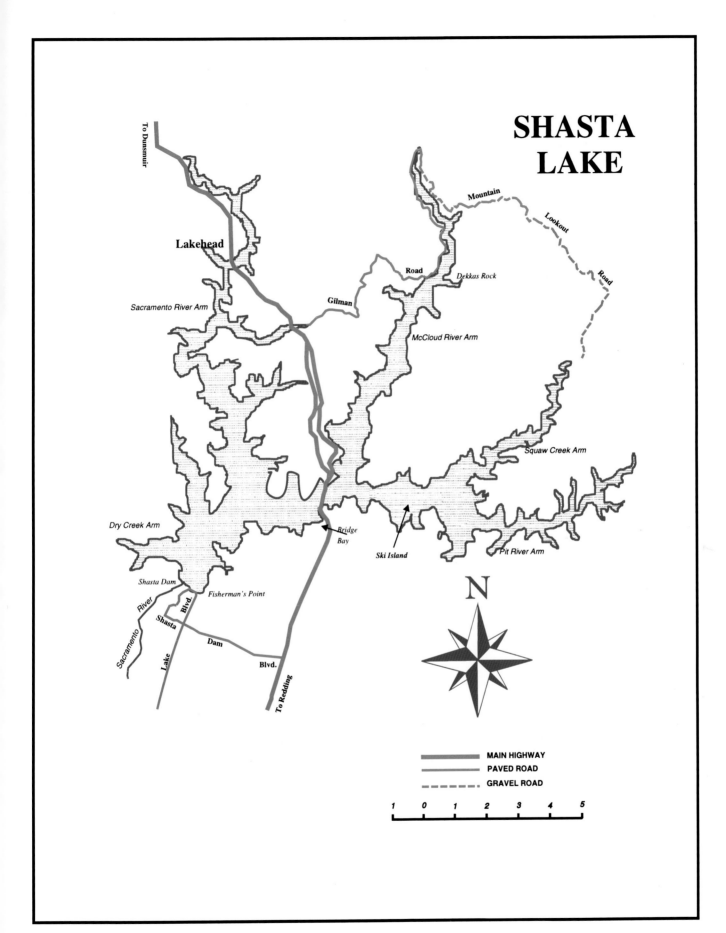

SHASTA LAKE

To Dunsmuir

Lakehead

Mountain

Lookout

Road

Dekkas Rock

Road

Sacramento River Arm

Gilman

McCloud River Arm

Squaw Creek Arm

Dry Creek Arm

Bridge Bay

Ski Island

Pit River Arm

Shasta Dam

Fisherman's Point

Sacramento River

Shasta

Blvd.

Lake

Dam

Blvd.

To Redding

N

MAIN HIGHWAY
PAVED ROAD
GRAVEL ROAD

1   0   1   2   3   4   5

There are all sorts of fish in huge Lake Shasta. This one is a Kamloops trout.

bass lake. It will never achieve the reputation enjoyed by Lake Shasta, Trinity Lake, or even nearby Lake Shastina, although I've seen smallmouth that top five pounds.

The best area for bank anglers to fish is along the north shore. Take W.A. Barr Road out of Mount Shasta and turn right onto North Shore Road. Follow it across Wagon Creek and along the lake where the road winds through the trees. Several undeveloped parking areas can be seen from the road. Park in any of them, bait up with a crawler, Power Bait or Pautzke Fireballs, cast the line out, and let it soak.

If trolling, a very hot technique is to tie a dark fly onto the monofilament with either very little or no weight and troll slowly, dragging the fly in the surface film.

Trollers also use small Rapalas and any of the various spinners and spoons on the market.

Shasta Lake

Shasta Lake is the largest reservoir in California. Although it is considered one of the finest bass lakes in the West, it doesn't have a great reputation for trout. Except for a small cadre of anglers, no one seems to take trout fishing seriously at Shasta Lake. People do not go to Shasta for the trout fishing, although they may hang a rod off the side of a houseboat once they get there.

Trout angling is best in early to late spring, while the lake surface is cool. Trophy trout to seven and eight pounds are caught often this time of year. During this period the trout feed near the surface on schools of threadfin shad, a tiny baitfish. As the lake surface warms, the trout are driven deeper to find cool water.

The trout fishing this time of year is unsophisticated as fishing techniques go. Most anglers use a bobber and a minnow. A Shur-Stop goes on the line first. This is a tiny piece of thin, flat metal a quarter-inch long with a hole in each end. The line goes through one hole, makes a wrap around the metal, then goes through the other hole. Its purpose is to allow the bobber to slide up or down the line to the length you want the bobber above the bait.

Tie on a barrel swivel to keep the bobber from sliding against the hook when casting. Hook the minnow behind the dorsal fin so it can swim around. A couple of split shot a foot or so above the hook will keep the minnow near the bottom. You can also use crayfish, crawlers, crickets or Power Bait.

The easiest area to fish from shore is near the dam, from Fishermen's Point on the south side to the Dry Creek arm on the north shore. As the lake surface warms and drives the fish deeper, trollers use downriggers to get Kastmasters and other shad imitations down to the fish, often to 80 feet or more.

Bank anglers can still fish with crawlers and minnows when fish are deep. Simply run the line down to the depth the fish are working. Much of the bank at Shasta Lake is very steep, so by casting out and letting the bait sink, anglers can get their bait down to almost any depth. The best fishing is in the main channel of the lake, from the lower reaches of the main arms to the dam.

Anglers fishing the Sacramento River arm will find the best fishing occurs from the O'Brien Creek Inlet downstream to the dam.

Anglers on the McCloud arm have the most success from the Shasta Caverns to the mouth on the main body of the lake. From the caverns back into the arm to Dekkas Rock, fishing is spotty. The McCloud is considered to be the best trout fishing arm on the lake. From the mouth of Squaw Creek and the Pit River to the McCloud River arm is where the biggest fish in the lake are generally caught—trout that run from two to six pounds are caught near Ski Island. A lot of nice fish are also caught in the Bridge Bay area.

Trout aren't the only fish in the lake—Shasta is well-known for small mouth spotted and black bass. It also has a healthy catfish population along with bluegill and crappie. An angler who was fishing near Ski Island in July of 1989 even landed a 173 1/2- pound sturgeon. Sturgeon have been landlocked in Shasta Lake since the dam was built in 1949. Anglers began fishing for them several years ago but success has been very limited. One long-time Shasta fisherman likes to tell the story of a time he went fishing and his rod began sliding into the water. He grabbed it but the 12-pound test line was running off the reel so fast he thought the drag was loose. By the time he tried to tighten the drag, the line came to the end and broke off. Then he tested the drag and found that it had been tightened down the whole time.

Access

Shasta Lake has 370 miles of shoreline, more than San Francisco Bay. To describe each fishing area would require a book in itself. But any place where you can walk to the water line and throw a line in could be as good as any other.

Fishermen's Point

To reach the dam, take Shasta Dam Boulevard/Central Valley Exit from I-5 four miles north of Redding. Stay on Shasta Dam Boulevard to the Lake Boulevard intersection and turn right. When you reach the lake, turn left toward the dam. You will come to a parking area and a sign marking Fishermen's Point fishing access. Park in the lot and take the trail down to the lake shore.

You can fish wherever the trail meets the water's edge or work back toward the dam where the shoreline is heavily rip-rapped with large boulders.

Although it is a tough climb, many anglers prefer the rip-rap area because crayfish, a favorite food source for trout and bass, can hide in the rocks.

Dry Creek Arm

Follow the road across the dam and turn to the right onto a gravel road. Follow it to an unimproved parking area. Fish off any of the points in this area or hike up the lake to the Dry Creek arm.

Sacramento River Arm

Drive north of Redding on Interstate 5 to Lakehead. You can turn onto Sugarloaf Road and fish down the Sacramento arm or turn right to Antlers and the public launch ramp.

McCloud River Arm

Continue north on I-5 to Salt Creek Road and turn right. Follow the road 17 miles along the McCloud arm, cross the McCloud River bridge and drive to the campground. When the lake level is low, this area of the McCloud is a free-flowing stream. Before you get excited, it is nothing at all like the famed Lower McCloud. Here, it is full of silt and is lifeless.

If the lake level is up, this area is stocked by the DFG. In fall, rainbows and browns congregate in the arm waiting to enter the stream to spawn.

Squaw Creek Arm

Continue on past the McCloud Bridge campground to where the road dead ends to reach the Squaw Creek arm. Little is known about fishing the lake in this area.

Pit River Arm

The Upper Pit River arm of Shasta Lake is virtually unreachable by vehicle.

Gary Morales sets up for early morning trolling on Lake Shasta.

.... Chapter Six

McCloud River

The McCloud River provides some of the best and toughest fishing in California. Nicole Gordon is high-stick nymphing, the most productive way to fish the McCloud.

The McCloud is the quintessential freestone stream, a year-round flow of clear, cold water coursing through a wild, lush canyon. The wild strain of rainbows in the McCloud are gallant, hard-fighting fish. And the river's fast-flowing character gives them little time to consider whether the fly passing through the feeding zone is natural or a deception.

The McCloud is recognized as having one of the finest strains of wild trout in the world. In the late 19th century, eggs taken from the Shasta strain of rainbows in the McCloud River were used to stock streams in the Eastern United States and ultimately streams throughout Europe. The hatchery where those eggs were taken, which was located near O'Brien, is now covered by the waters of Shasta Lake.

In exchange for the rainbows, brown trout from Europe were stocked in the McCloud. Although the McCloud is noted for its rainbow fishery, its brown trout population is a giant that has finally awoken. As the McCloud Dam tamed the flows of the lower river, the stream bed began to channelize, creating the long, slow pools that big browns thrive in.

Each fall, browns migrate into the upper reaches of the Lower McCloud to spawn. Huge browns to 10 pounds and more hold in the upper river until their eggs ripen. Then, with

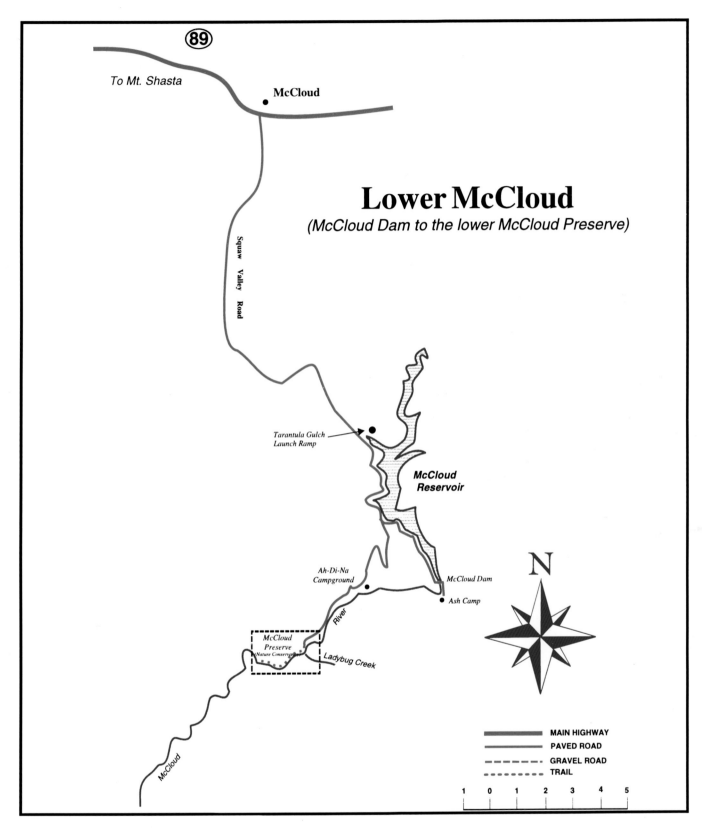

89

To Mt. Shasta

McCloud

Lower McCloud
(McCloud Dam to the lower McCloud Preserve)

Squaw Valley Road

Tarantula Gulch Launch Ramp

McCloud Reservoir

Ah-Di-Na Campground

McCloud Dam

Ash Camp

McCloud Preserve (Nature Conservancy)

River

Ladybug Creek

McCloud

N

	MAIN HIGHWAY
	PAVED ROAD
	GRAVEL ROAD
	TRAIL

1 0 1 2 3 4 5

powerful thrusts of their tails, they dig into the gravel and deposit their eggs before returning to the lower end of the river and lake. Because great numbers of the browns spawn in the McCloud, fishing in late fall is the best time to be on the river.

The McCloud also was the southernmost habitat for Dolly Varden, which haven't been seen in the river for two decades.

The Lower McCloud River

McCloud Dam was built in the mid-1960s to divert water from the McCloud River through a tunnel to the Pit River. When the lake opened to fishing in 1966, catching a limit of 10 rainbows was simple. Fishing from a boat anchored near the lake's conflu-ence with the river we often caught our limit of trout by 10 a.m.

and headed for home. Fishing pressure on the reservoir has made fishing very tough since then.

Before the road to Ah-Di-Na Campground was opened to the public, the only way in to the Lower McCloud was to pack in. The Lower McCloud was the southernmost habitat for Dolly Varden, a char related to the trout family. Whenever McCloud locals hiked into Ah-Di-Na for a two- or three-day stay, someone in the party invariably caught a large Dolly Varden.

Water diversions drastically lowered the flows of the river and controlled releases consequently destroyed the deep pools necessary to the Dolly's survival. Dolly Varden haven't been documented in the McCloud River since 1975, although it continues to be a fine stream for rainbows and browns.

Angling regulations on this part of the river allow fishing only with artificial lures and barbless hooks. Although almost everyone practices catch-and-release, there is a two-fish limit from McCloud Dam downstream to Lady Bug Creek, and a zero limit below Lady Bug Creek.

At one time a private club, the McCloud River Club, owned all of the property bordering the McCloud River from Ah-Di-Na Campground down to the river's confluence with Shasta Lake. When the road to Ah-Di-Na made the Lower McCloud accessible to the public, poaching and trespassing became a problem the McCloud River Club was unable to deal with. To create a buffer zone between the club and the public, several miles of the uppermost property was donated to the Nature Conservancy, an environmental organization. This area is now the McCloud Preserve.

Today, the Conservancy allows a controlled number of anglers onto the upper part of their river for fishing. The lower portion remains closed to the public.

A policy of the McCloud Preserve contends that man is a visitor to the preserve and must respect the rights of other living creatures to live in peace. Killing or harming any animal, even the rattlesnakes in the area, is forbidden. Those rules are made clear as you enter the property. If they offend you, go elsewhere.

As you enter the property, sign the book at the caretaker's cabin, where Conservancy volunteers are on duty. The Conservancy allows 10 visitors, whether they be anglers or non-anglers, on the property at one time. If those spots are full, you may wait until someone leaves. In the past, getting onto the preserve was relatively easy. Today, you will probably need reservations to fish the preserve on a weekend.

The McCloud Preserve constitutes only a portion of the fishable water of the Lower McCloud. You can also fish the excellent waters from Ah-Di-Nah Campground down to the upper boundary of the preserve, or by crossing the dam, you can fish upriver, from the McCloud Dam down past Ash Camp, another exceptional bit of water.

Fishing the Lower McCloud

The McCloud River has one of the most consistent flows of any stream in California. Shortly below Fowler's Campground, mountain snowmelt gushes from springs along the river banks and is ice-cold year-round. This area, called Big Springs, is on the Hearst Estate and is closed to the public.

These flows tumble freely along from Big Springs downstream to the river's confluence with McCloud Reservoir. Although a minimum flow is allowed to continue down the Lower McCloud past the dam, most of the McCloud River is diverted through a tunnel to a powerhouse on the Pit River.

Before the road to Ah-Di-Na Campground on the Lower

McCloud was opened by the U.S. Forest Service, the lower river was inaccessible unless the angler was willing to make a long hike in.

Spring

The river from the dam downstream to Ash Camp at the mouth of Hawkins Creek becomes low very early in the season. This is because the gauging station is at Ah-Di-Na Campground, four miles downstream. Water from side streams gives the gauge enough water so that water releases from the dam must meet only minimal flows.

In mid-May the McCloud often is one of the few streams that can be fished while others are washed out. Fred Gordon, a Dunsmuir fishing guide, has fished the McCloud River since it became available to the public. Gordon says that he's never seen the McCloud unfishable in all the years that he's fished it. Even on the rare occasion when it does get washed out, it doesn't stay out for long.

Gordon fishes the McCloud differently than he does the Pit or the Upper Sacramento River. The McCloud has large rocks and deep pools, and very little gravel along the river's edge. In some of the deeper pools, he will use a yarn indicator with as much as eight feet of 5X tippet, and a piece of split shot at the end of the tippet. The really deep, slow pools are more like fishing a lake than a river, so he uses smaller patterns, usually Prince Nymphs, a Sparkle PT Nymph or Bird's Nest. If the pool is a little faster he may go up to a size 14, dropping to size 18s if the pool is slow.

Although he considers the McCloud a better stream for nymphing than for fishing dries, Gordon is always prepared with an assortment of Parachute Adams, Cahills and Stimulators, in case the fish key to a particular hatch.

By mid-May to early June, Little Sally stone dries can be good at midday. By mid-June the dry-fly fishing is only in the evenings, with the last hour or two of daylight the best fishing.

Gordon says to watch for large mayflies, size 8 and 10, and some small *Baetis*, size 16 and 18.

"The Elk Hair Caddis and Parachute Adams in size 14 are some of my favorite dry flies," says Gordon, "especially in fast water." In pools where the fish are more finicky, the imitations must be better, including using a Paradun to imitate a mayfly.

The evening dry-fly activity is sporadic. Even when there is an abundance of surface activity the fish may not be moving for them.

Summer

With the hot weather of midsummer, the McCloud sometimes becomes clouded with glacial silt from the slopes of nearby Mount Shasta. This is primarily a matter of aesthetics, however, and the fishing can be even more productive because the fish are made less wary by the decrease in visibility. In this situation, Gordon sticks with size 14 Bead Head Prince Nymphs, Bead Head Zug Bugs, Bird's Nests and the Flashback AP Nymphs. If dry flies are coming off, he will switch to size 14 Parachute Adams or Cahills in this situation.

Normally during summer Gordon works the McCloud as he would any other river, concentrating on the bubble curtains and riffles, where the fish can pick up oxygen. One thing that he has noticed is that the mornings are generally slow, but the fishing picks up again in the afternoon. If you don't catch fish in the morning, stick it out, and wait for the fish to turn on.

Although the water in the Lower McCloud remains cold throughout the summer, the hatches continue to be pushed back in the day until they come off in the waning moments of daylight.

Fall

October Caddis

Gordon believes that the McCloud is a better stream for fishing the October caddis hatch than the Sacramento because the canyon is narrower and the foliage hangs right over the river. This keeps the caddis closer to the river and the fish seem to key on them better.

Although the conditions for October caddis are better on the McCloud, Gordon has noted that the fish seem to react to them the same way. "The fish don't seem to key on the October caddis until they have mated, made their egg-laying flights, retired to the overgrowth along the river, and fallen in." At this point, Gordon casts a size 2 to size 8 Stimulator or Goddard Caddis under the overhanging foliage to fish working the dead or dying insects. Of course, the angler who is lucky enough to be on the stream when the insects emerge and buzz across the stream toward shore can also expect great fishing on the dries, but this is seldom happens.

Brown Trout

If there is an early winter, with some rain and snow in late fall, you should see brown trout moving around the tailouts of the pools. Look for cleaned spots of gravel, an indication that browns are in the pool. You may not see them, but they will be there and may be holding at the head of the pool, usually in five to ten feet of water.

Gordon handles this situation by going to the head of the pool and running a size 14 to 16 Prince Nymph or Black AP Nymph through the pool right along the bottom.

Some pools are fished with streamers, those where the tailouts are five feet deep or so. Gordon rigs a sinking line, a short leader and a size 8 Leech in black, brown or dark brown, casting it across, mending the line upstream as the fly sinks, then allowing the fly to swing across the current near the tail of the pool.

If you hit the magic moment when the fish are spawning, cast an egg pattern, a champagne colored Glo Bug, behind the redds and the fish will take it. Even if you are fishing for rainbows, the key is to get the Glo Bug behind the spawning ground.

Accessing the Lower McCloud

Mile 0.0: Intersection of Squaw Valley Creek Road and Highway 89. Turn south on Southern Avenue past the Shell station and keep going. The road takes you through Squaw Valley and becomes Squaw Valley Creek Road.

Mile 9.0: Tarantula Gulch. The road leaves the valley and climbs a steep mountain ridge before descending as steeply to McCloud Reservoir and a well-developed boat ramp and parking area. To reach the Lower McCloud River follow Forest Service road to the right.

Mile 11.3: The turnoff to Ah-Di-Na and the McCloud Preserve is marked by a sign on the right. Ah-Di-Na, a Forest Service Campground, is a six-mile climb and descent over a steep ridge.

Mile 17.2: Ah-Di-Na Campground is a Forest Service Campground on the McCloud River. It has no showers, but remains quite busy through the summer. The fishing from here upstream or downstream is typical of the balance of this river. The river is lush with foliage, and the pools are long and well-defined.

Mile 18.2: McCloud Preserve. Follow the road past Ah-Di-Na Campground approximately one mile to where it dead ends. The Nature Conservancy property begins at the creek at the end of the road. Cross the foot bridge and continue along a very

Bead Head Prince Nymph. The Prince Nymph is an effective nymph pattern on streams throughout California.

primitive trail to the Caretaker's Cabin at Lady Bug Creek. You must sign in at a registration book on the side of the cabin. Although fishing the preserve is a privilege, the entire Lower McCloud is excellent fishing and it would be deceptive to rate one stretch of it over another.

Mile 13.3: McCloud Dam. Instead of turning off to Ah-Di-Na, stay on USFS #11 and follow the road around the lake to where it crosses McCloud Dam. Cross the dam then turn right to access the Lower McCloud from the dam down to Ash Camp.

Mile 13.8: Water Gauging Station. Half a mile below the dam, a pipe rail follows a trail to a gauging station, about 150 yards below the road. Once on the river, an undeveloped trail provides access for several hundred yards upstream and downstream from the gauging station. This is a beautiful stretch of river, with long pools and short, fast pockets of water. An afternoon here when the mayflies are hatching can be tantalizing as well as entertaining when rising fish, which are very particular about patterns they will accept, sip the duns from the surface.

Mile 14.2: Hawkins Creek and Ash Camp. A gravel road drops off to the right into an undeveloped camping area where Hawkins Creek empties into the McCloud. The Pacific Crest Trail crosses the river here on a suspended foot bridge. You can follow the trail down river to Ah-Di-Na campground.

This area is typical of the Lower McCloud, lush plant life in a deep canyon. The river current rushes over huge boulders, making wading a challenging prospect, nevertheless providing excellent fishing. The holes in this area are not as well defined as those at Ah-Di-Na and through the McCloud Preserve.

For More Information
Guide Fred Gordon
(530) 235-2673

The Fly Shop
(530) 222-3555

Dunsmuir Fly Shop
(530) 235-0705

Chapter Seven

Hat Creek

Hat Creek, the first restored wild trout stream in California, is a combination of spring-creek-like slicks and a few riffles.

The trophy section of lower Hat Creek, one of the most popular stretches of trout water in California, provides an excellent model of what a stream can be when forces come together to make it happen.

Lower Hat Creek, that area of the stream from the Hat No. 2 Powerhouse downstream to Lake Britton, started with the potential of becoming great trout water. According to Steve Vaughn, owner of Vaughn's Sporting Goods in Burney, the stream has always had big trout. But it also had a healthy population of rough fish—suckers and squawfish that made their way into the river from Lake Britton.

In 1968, the Burney and San Francisco chapters of Trout Unlimited, along with the state Department of Fish and Game, Pacific Gas & Electric and the Wildlife Conservation Board came together to create the first trophy trout stream in California.

A barrier dam was constructed above the stream's confluence with Lake Britton. Then the Department of Fish and Game trapped as many native trout as they could, put them in a holding pond, and poisoned the stream. With the rough fish cleared out, Hat Creek was restocked with the native browns and rainbows that had been trapped.

The regulations for Hat Creek were changed, including catch restrictions and limiting

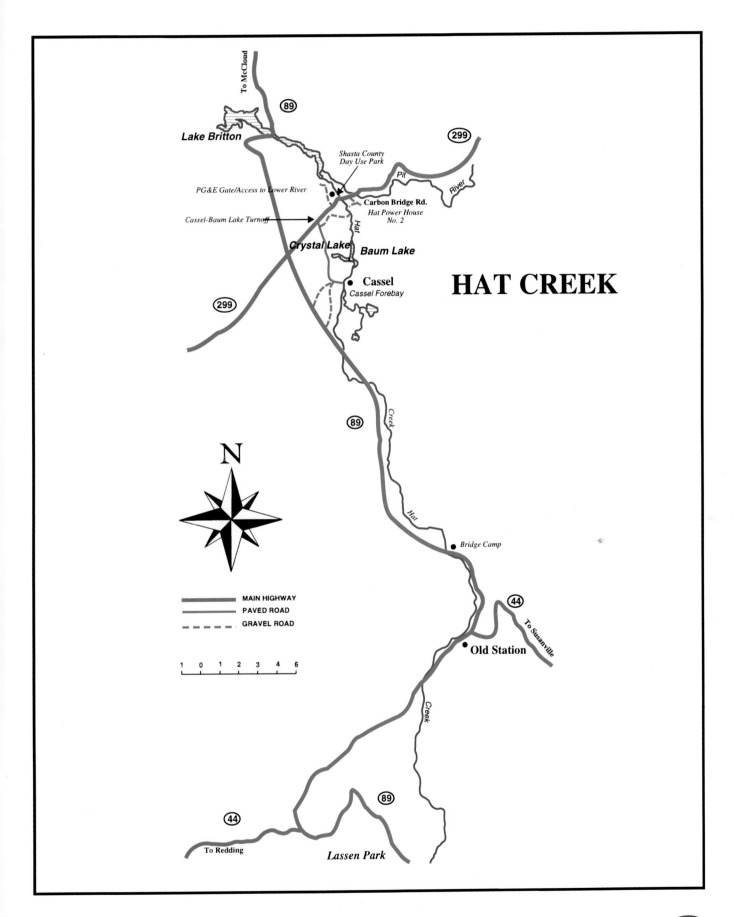

To McCloud

89

Lake Britton

299

Shasta County
Day Use Park

Pit

River

PG&E Gate/Access to Lower River

Carbon Bridge Rd.
Hat Power House
No. 2

Cassel-Baum Lake Turnoff

Crystal Lake   Baum Lake

HAT CREEK

Hat

Cassel

Cassel Forebay

299

N

MAIN HIGHWAY
PAVED ROAD
GRAVEL ROAD

1 0 1 2 3 4 6

89

Creek

Hat

Bridge Camp

44

To Susanville

Old Station

Creek

89

44

To Redding   Lassen Park

tackle to artificial lures with barbless hooks. Since then, the trout population has relied on natural propagation to regenerate itself. The stream hasn't been stocked in nearly 30 years and today this three-mile stretch of Hat Creek is one of the most popular stretches of river in the state.

The Wild Trout Area

Hat Number Two Powerhouse downstream to Lake Britton

"Hat Creek is a stream that will test your knowledge of insects, your ability to present a fly, and test every other skill that you have as a fly angler," says Andy Burk, an accomplished fly tier and excellent fly fisher. "The person who is seeking that level of a challenge will find few places in California that offer it as well as Hat Creek."

Andy Burk is also a regular contributor to *California Fly Fisher* magazine as well as other publications. He is currently writing a book on innovative fly-tying techniques.

"Hat Creek has more varieties of mayflies, caddis, midges and stoneflies than most us can keep track of," says Burk. "It also has a variety of water types, from that of traditional English chalk streams with heavy weed growth to western freestone streams, and each with its own variety of insects.

"The way to up your odds on Hat Creek," according to Burk, "is to have a lot of imitations to draw from. In the course of a day you may fish 15 or 20 different flies. On the Lower Sac, you may fish four or five different patterns but they're essentially the same insect. On Hat Creek you might start in the morning with a size 22 Trico, move on to a size 4 Stonefly at midday, then a size 16 Caddis, and finish the day with a size 10 or 12 Green Drake.

You can tell a serious Hat Creek angler by his fly box, it will be stuffed with the broadest array of mayfly, caddis, midge and stone imitations that you've ever seen, from size 4 Golden Stones right down to size 22 and 24 Western Olive Mayflies."

The Powerhouse Riffle

The top of the Wild Trout area is Powerhouse Two. The Powerhouse Riffle, 150 to 200 yards long, is probably the most popular water on Hat Creek because this area has a lot of food which attracts a lot of fish.

According to Burk, both high-stick nymphing and nymphing under an indicator are productive in this area because of its diverse array of insects. Among these are golden stones, salmonflies, giant stones, little yellow stones, the little olive stones, and later in the fall, another golden stone which is about a size 12 or 14, as opposed to the size 4 or 6 giant golden stones.

This area also has a tremendous variety of mayflies, pale morning duns, rusty quills, *Paraleptophlebia*, Tricos and blue-wing olives.

Fly Patterns

For nymphing in this area, Burk recommends the size 12 to 18 Hare's Ears, Bird's Nests, HBI Nymphs, Epoxy Back PMDs, and size 6 to 10 Epoxy Back Golden Stones. Among the caddis patterns are the Z Wing Caddis and the LaFontaine Caddis Pupa. Dry patterns include: size 14 to 16 Paraduns, Light Cahills, and Adams; size 14 to 18 Elk Hair Caddis; size 8 to 10 Stimulators for when the big stoneflies are coming off. For the mayflies, Burk uses size 14 to 18 Mayfly Emergers.

Even though it's a riffle, the Powerhouse area has an abundance of weed growth, so it also has a variety of slow-water

insects, like the pale morning dun. There are five or six varieties of caddis and midges, which are really important later in the season, particularly during the dog days of August. For these insects, Burk uses size 14 to 18 PMDs, Rusty Quills, Tricos and Blue-wing Olives.

There is a saying on Hat Creek that the easy fish to catch are at the Powerhouse Riffle. Someone once suggested putting a sign on the oak tree that sits at the lower edge of the riffle: *Beginners*, with an arrow pointing upstream, and *Experts*, with an arrow pointing downstream. He said if he put that sign up, people wouldn't fish the Powerhouse anymore.

Powerhouse Riffle on Hat Creek is an extremely popular fishing area. And with good reason—there are an incredible number of fish caught (and released) at this spot.

Fly Patterns for the Powerhouse Riffle

For nymphing in this area, Burk recommends the size 12 to 18 Hare's Ears, Bird's Nests, HBI Nymphs, Epoxy Back PMDs, and size 6 to 10 Epoxy Back Golden Stones. Among the caddis patterns are the Z Wing Caddis and the LaFontaine Caddis Pupa. Dry patterns include: size 14 to 16 Paraduns, Light Cahills, and Adams; size 14 to 18 Elk Hair Caddis; size 8 to 10 Stimulators when the big stoneflies are coming off. For the mayflies, Burk uses size 14 to 18 Mayfly Emergers. Use size 14 to 18 PMDs, Rusty Quills, Tricos and Blue-wing Olives when the fish are taking dries.

The Meadows

As the stream starts to slow down and become more of a chalk stream it becomes a more diverse fishery. This is beautiful water to fish, with Hat Creek meandering through two miles of rolling hills and meadows. For the most part there isn't a lot of brush or trees along the river's edge, giving a clear back cast. But it's the toughest fishing because the clear water provides the trout with good visibility, and it's an educated trout population.

The insects in this area are mostly mayflies and midges, and include the flat- or slow-water species—the blue-wing olives, Tricos, pale morning duns and green drakes. There are consistent hatches of mayflies in the morning, and then again in the evening, although at times they can also come off at midday.

You can do some nymphing during the midday periods, you just have to fish deeper. A competent indicator nymph fisher, or a competent high-sticker, can do just as well as during the hatches. After the excitement of the morning hatch, however, most anglers are willing to take a break.

The meadows stretch has such a diverse array of insects that we recommend that you stop at a local fly shop or hire a local guide, at least for the first time or two in that area.

But some of the standard patterns are the Pale Morning Duns, Blue-wing Olives and Tricos. If you are on the river in May or June, then come prepared for the green drakes, especially on a blustery day.

The Lower Riffles

The lower riffles are located below the day park, downstream from Highway 299. This riffle section doesn't have as large a population of fish as it looks like it should have, but it does hold a lot of fish. There are certain pockets that they favor.

A variety of nymphs will work in this area, mostly size 10 to 16 Bird's Nests, Hare's Ears and Golden Stones, and size 12 to 16 Bead Head Prince Nymphs. Also come prepared with some of the smaller mayfly nymphs like the size 14 to 18 HBI Nymphs and the Epoxy Back PMDs. If you are there in late May or early June, be prepared for the *Pteronarcys* (salmonfly) hatch with a size 2 to 4 Goddard Caddis or other stonefly imitations.

Upper Hat Creek

Lassen Park to Hwy. 89

Hat Creek is accessible to the public where it follows Highway 44 from Big Pine Campground downstream to Old Station, then turns to follow Highway 89 west to Bridge Campground. From there it enters private property where access is not allowed. The only other public access is at Honn Campground.

This upper portion of Hat Creek is a freestone stream, fed by snowmelt from the slopes of Lassen Peak. It is heavily stocked with hatchery rainbows and offers good bait and lure fishing water where the quality of fishing is directly related to the last visit by the hatchery truck.

On the other hand, there are no special regulations or pretensions. According to Steve Vaughn, owner of Vaughn's Sporting Goods, a Burney landmark for outdoorsmen visiting California's Intermountain area, a kid with a spinning rod and a jar of salmon eggs can be just as successful as a veteran fly angler.

This is a great stream for anglers with spinning rods to toss lures—Panther Martins, Mepps Spinners and Rooster Tails— any kind of spinner with a light blade.

Upper Hat Creek also offers decent fly fishing, although most fly rodders tend to concentrate on the wild trout area in the lower river. If you happen to be in this area, try fishing the pocket water and areas not necessarily worked by spin anglers. Try nymphing with size 10 to 12 Zug Bugs, Hare's Ears and AP Nymphs. If you're motivated to fish with dries, use size 12 to 14 Adams' or Humpies.

"These fish also respond to Woolly Buggers and attractor patterns," says Vaughn. "Cast up and across the stream, then strip back so the fly darts across the current, particularly in the early mornings and late evenings."

Upper Hat Creek is a good place to introduce someone to fly fishing. There is little danger of someone who may be a bit sensitive about his or her ability to form a perfect loop, who can't

react to a strike without putting a fly into the trees overhead, and who doesn't know that *Callibaetis* is another word for mayfly, becoming intimidated by the "Two thousand dollars on the hoof" crowd.

Where Hat Creek leaves the national forest it enters private property and access to the stream is severely restricted.

Cassel Forebay

Cassel to Baum Lake

Rising River converges with Hat Creek near Cassel, and transforms Hat Creek from a freestone stream into a spring creek. Although all of Rising River flows through private property, the transformation is obvious, and at this point, Hat Creek, in actuality, becomes a tributary of Rising River, although the name of the stream implies just the opposite.

"This area can be dynamite," says Vaughn, "although not all fish are trophies." A few years ago, however, Vaughn caught a 24-inch, seven-pound rainbow in this area on a size 16 Adams.

Bait anglers can also fish the Cassel area, using crickets, night crawlers and salmon eggs as effectively as fly anglers use nymphs and dries. Lures also work well, as do small Rapalas, and especially the bladed spinners such as Panther Martins and Kastmasters.

Fly fishing Cassel Forebay is much the same as fishing the flat water of lower Hat Creek. Fish stonefly nymphs in the early season, then switch to the smaller pale morning duns, pale evening duns and caddis as the weather warms.

Baum Lake

"Baum Lake has all the characteristics of a spring creek, and should be fished like a wide spot on Hat Creek," says Vaughn. Baum Lake is heavily stocked by the DFG with fish from Crystal Creek Hatchery.

The powerhouse at Baum Lake is good for bait and lure fishing, but tough for fly anglers. Once you get below the bridge and into the main flow of the lake, fly fishing improves as does the other techniques.

"The hatchery outlet is a cove where fish migrate in and out," says Vaughn. "This area can be good for bait and for lures. Fly fishing is good in the flats along the big curve toward the parking area at the eastern point, but lure and bait fishing is tough because of the aquatic growth. The outlet of Crystal Lake is a large bay that is good for all fishing techniques," says Vaughn. As the waters join, they form a current that flows toward the main body of Baum Lake. This is a good area for trolling with electric motors, since gas engines aren't allowed on Baum Lake. It's also a good area for fly fishing.

Beyond that is the narrows where the lake becomes deeper. This is a good area for larger fish. The main body of the lake is where most of the fly anglers fish, either from shore, from a boat or from a float tube. Most of the fishing in this area is with nymphs, leeches, Matukas and Woolly Worms in olive or black, retrieved with short twitches along the bottom.

Baum Lake also gets its share of hatches, primarily from flat-water insects, like pale morning duns, *Callibaetis* mayflies and numerous varieties of caddis. During winter the midges are the predominant hatch, and Vaughn advises using Midge Emergers or Midge Pupae, fished on sinking lines or under an indicator. During summer the *Callibaetis* will come off at midday, and some little yellow stones in the evening. In the evenings during summer and fall, caddis will come off toward dusk.

Access

The junction of Highways 299 and 89 will be the point of origin for Hat Creek access routes.

Mile 0.0: The junction of Highways 299 and 89 can be reached two ways. Take the Highway 299 East exit from Interstate 5 just north of Redding (don't be confused by the Highway 299 West Exit about two miles to the south) and follow Highway 299 east to Burney. Two miles past Burney, Highway 299 intersects with Highway 89.

Another route further to the north is to take Highway 89 at the McCloud Exit of I-5, just south of Mount Shasta City. Follow Highway 89 east through the town of McCloud and on about 50 miles to the Highway 299/Highway 89 intersection. A left turn onto Highway 299 goes north to lower Hat Creek, a right turn goes to Burney. Straight ahead will take you to upper Hat Creek.

Cassel

Mile 2.1: Cassel-Baum Lake Turnoff. The Cassel Road leads to the Cassel Forebay, Baum Lake and Crystal Lake.

Turn right onto Cassel Road. The Baum Lake/Crystal Creek Hatchery is 2.1 miles in on Cassel Road. Turn left and drive one mile to the hatchery. Baum Lake is to the left with a large parking area.

At mile 3.5 Cassel Road crosses Hat Creek at the Cassel Forebay. A camping and parking area on the left parallels the channel of the forebay.

The Trophy Trout Section

Mile 2.7: Hat Creek Powerhouse No. 2. From the junction of Highways 89 and 299, continue north 2.7 miles to a road on the right marked "Hat No. 2." This is the PG&E access road to Hat Creek Powerhouse No. 2. At this point the water from Baum Lake that was diverted to the powerhouse several miles downstream reenters the river.

At the parking area near the powerhouse, a sign in a kiosk describes the efforts that went into creating California's first trophy-trout stream.

The first piece of water is the Powerhouse Riffle. Below that the stream enters the meadows, where Hat Creek becomes a classic spring creek with long, glassy pools. It winds its way through the rolling hills in banks lined with cattails and tall grass, a rich contrast to the dry, rolling hills that surround Hat Creek.

This is the Hat Creek that challenges the angler head on, requiring long, gossamer leaders and perfect, drag-free, dead-drift, dry-fly presentations or nymph fishing with indicators.

Mile 3.4: PG&E Gate. This offers access to the riffle section, the barrier dam and the stream's confluence with Lake Britton.

On the left side of Highway 299, a green metal gate marks the PG&E access road to the lower river. Several side roads lead off, but keep bearing to the right for 0.7 mile to a fork in the road. Take the right fork onto a meadow and another fence. A path through a gate leads downriver, a fork to the right ends at another fence. Park here to fish your way upriver.

The lower riffle section of Hat Creek runs from just above the fence downstream to the barrier dam. From the fence upstream to the county park the stream has little character. Fish in this area hide beneath undercut banks or around the occasional fallen tree that is buried in the limestone silt.

Mile 3.7: Shasta County Picnic Area. Although fishing is legal at the Shasta County Park and picnic area, few people seem to bother.

This part of the stream is like the others, a limestone streambed covered with aquatic weeds. One can sit at one of the picnic tables enjoying a cold drink on a warm summer evening and watch trout rise for an endless variety of mayflies and caddis.

Mile 3.8: Bridge Over Hat Creek. A short distance past the Shasta County Park is a cattle pen and loading chute on the right side of Highway 299. The road to the upper section of Hat Creek goes through the gate, past the pen and winds away from the stream. Be sure to close the gate behind you.

Mile 4.2: Carbon Bridge Road. When you come to a fork in the road, bear to the right and you will come to the parking area at the site of the old Carbon Bridge. The left fork comes to a dead end on private property.

The road ends in the heart of the meadow section, where Hat Creek meanders over a limestone streambed with an abundance of aquatic weeds. The stream flow is undisturbed by boulders. This area, like the pools below Hat Powerhouse No. 2, consists of long, smooth pools, requiring exquisite downstream presentations.

The white tuft on the Parachute Adams makes it an ideal pattern to use during the low light of evening hatches.

For More Information
The Fly Shop
Churn Creek Road
Redding, CA 96003
(530) 222-3555

Vaughn's Sporting Goods
P.O. Box 2690
Burney, CA 96013
(530) 335-2381

Chapter Eight

Trinity River

A bald eagle scoops a trout from the surface of Lewiston Lake.

Although the Trinity River is better known as a steelhead and salmon stream, it also has a significant brown trout fishery in the main stem of the river below Lewiston Dam. Some of the tributaries of the Trinity, those in the Trinity Alps, also offer unique fishing opportunities. The best trout fishing in the Trinity River watershed, in our opinion, however, is Lewiston Lake. Over the years, Lewiston Lake has developed the character of a spring creek, with predictable hatches and surprisingly sizable fish.

The brown trout fishery of the Trinity no longer enjoys the reputation it had through the 1970s and into the early 1980s.

Brown trout are not native to North America. They were brought here from Europe in exchange for rainbow trout in the late 19th century. The browns in the Trinity are the Loch Leven variety from Scotland rather than the German browns that are so common in the Western United States.

The Loch Leven are called sea trout in Europe because they are anadromous. Hatching from eggs in the river, they go to sea for a year or so, enjoying the rich food supply and growing at a much faster rate than they would in the stream. Ultimately, however, they do return to the stream to spawn as trophy-sized fish.

TRINITY RIVER

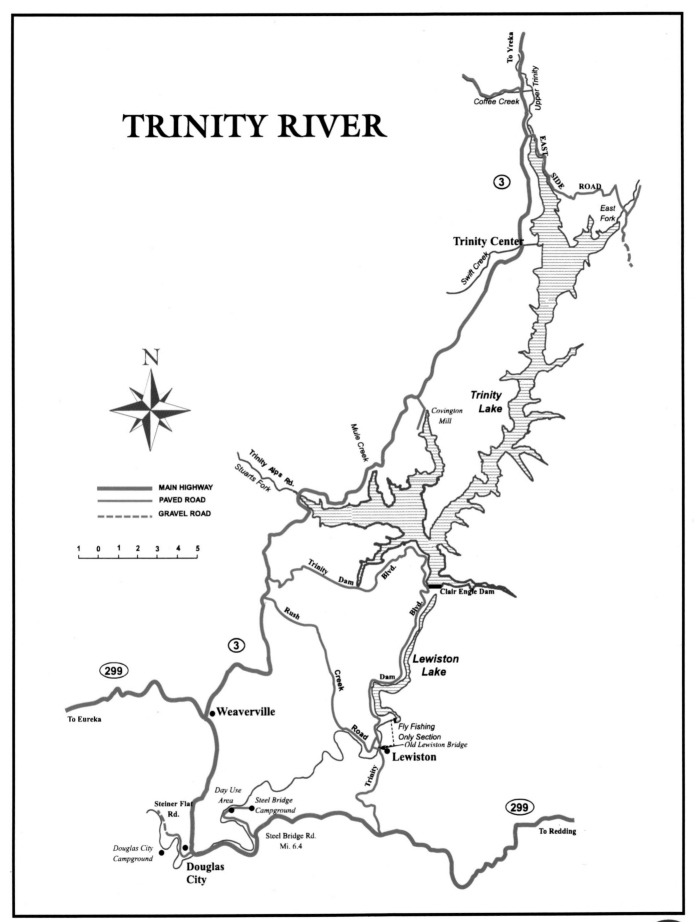

When Trinity Dam was built, several hundred miles of prime spawning habitat were closed to the salmon, steelhead and Loch Leven browns. When the lake behind the dam began to fill in 1961, the flows down the Trinity River were reduced to 150 cubic feet per second.

Without normal flows to flush silt out of the streambed, gravel in the lower Trinity began to cement in, making spawning difficult for the salmon and steelhead.

The main fisheries of the river, the salmon and steelhead, were reduced to near extinction. The browns, which had been maintained as a stocked fishery, were then blamed by the water agencies as the culprit for the low salmon and steelhead runs, as though the loss of habitat and low flows had nothing to do with it.

The brown trout stocking program was finally brought to a halt in 1978. Yet the browns continued to flourish until the early 1980s, then began to decline.

The brown trout fishery today is a remnant population that has residualized; that is, they are now mostly resident river fish. The population is very low, but they continue to hang on and provide fishing for those willing to work for them. Unfortunately for the brown trout population, people who catch the big fish, the spawners, tend to kill them for the freezer. We encourage everyone to release all browns caught in the Trinity.

The tributaries of the Trinity above Trinity Lake also enjoy good trout fishing in late spring and again in the fall.

The construction of the two dams on the river did benefit anglers in other ways. Trinity and Lewiston lakes have established themselves as unique fisheries in their own right.

Fishing Techniques: Fly Fishing

The Trinity River immediately below Lewiston Dam is a fly-fishing-only area that extends about two miles downstream to the Old Lewiston Bridge. This area is open to fishing from the last Saturday in April through September 15, and fishing may be done with flies only, whether on fly rods or spinning gear. Currently this is a zero limit area and Trinity County's only catch-and-release fishery.

Herb Burton, owner of Trinity Fly Shop and Guide Service in Lewiston, has been fishing the Trinity River system for the past 26 years. Burton has fished the Trinity watershed from the alpine lakes that feed the tributaries to the confluence with the Klamath River.

Burton says the brown trout extend from Lewiston to Del Loma, about 60 miles downstream. But the bulk of the fish are concentrated in the upper 20 miles, above Junction City, and for the purposes of this book, will include water from Lewiston Dam down to Steel Bridge Road.

Early in the season, the hatchery at Lewiston releases the juvenile salmon and steelhead into the river just below the Lewiston Dam and for a while the waters are boiling with these tiny fish. The browns move in to the river just below the hatchery and feast on these small fish until they move downstream and out of that stretch of water. While the juvenile fish are in this area, Burton uses streamers that simulate steelhead or salmon fry.

The river also has a large population of lamprey eels. Dark leech patterns such as Woolly Buggers and Olive or Black Matukas and Marabou Leech patterns are productive.

When the season opens, little golden stones populate the tailwater of the pools. Use similar golden stone imitations in size 8 through 12. The Lewiston area also has salmonflies (*Pteronarcys californica*) that can provide excellent late spring dry-fly action, but further downriver you will encounter fewer of these giant stoneflies.

Early in the season, streamers will generally take the biggest fish—most run from 14 to 19 inches with an occasional fish from three to six pounds. As the season progresses, golden stones become the most productive, fished dead and deep.

In late summer, an intense but brief caddis hatch occurs late in the evenings. The most common is the gray caddis that's indigenous to almost every river system in the West, but an olive caddis hatch also occurs at this time.

Fish the caddis hatch with caddis nymphs and what Burton calls Dirty Black Emergers, (DBEs). When fish obviously take adult caddis off the surface, fish Elk Hair Caddis dries.

At this time of year, even streamers fished in the late evening and early morning are productive.

Lures and Bait

Below the Old Lewiston Bridge, lures probably catch more browns than flies or bait. Specifically back-trolled Hot Shots and

Wee Warts, fished by drift-boat anglers for salmon or steelhead.

Bank anglers can fish spinners, either Panther Martins or Little Cleos. Fish these by casting the lure across the river and letting it swing across the current, then retrieve it upstream along the seam between the main current and the eddy along the bank. Or cast upstream and retrieve quickly down past the boulders that line the head of the pool.

Bait fishermen catch most of the browns while fishing the deep pools for salmon or steelhead. Although salmon anglers have better luck on the Trinity fishing with tuna balls, the occasional incidental brown is caught on salmon or steelhead roe.

Night crawlers are also a good bait for browns. The artificial baits, such as Power Bait, do not work as well.

Streams of the Trinity Alps

A great fishing experience is composed of a variety of factors, and although the tributaries of the Trinity River don't hold fish the size of the McCloud or the Lower Sacramento, they do offer solitude in lovely surroundings, and for the most part, relatively easy access.

Historically, the streams featured here were spawning streams for the salmon and steelhead of the Trinity River. When Clair Engle and Lewiston dams were built in the late 1950s, the anadromous runs of these fish were prevented from returning to these streams. On the other hand, the juveniles that were still in the stream were also prevented from migrating downstream to the ocean. Consequently, these fish adapted to the new environment and managed to become resident fish in streams that were more hospitable to migrating fish.

Joe Mercier of Canyon Flyfishing in Weaverville has fished the streams of the Trinity Alps for years, as well as the main stem of the Trinity River. Mercier has studied the stream from

Dale Lackey fishing the Trinity River.

a naturalist's and an ecologist's point of view, as well as from a fisherman's.

Although each stream in the Alps has qualities that make it unique, they all share some common characteristics: Each empties into Trinity Lake; each is used as a spawning stream for the lake's population of rainbows in the spring and summer; each is used for spawning by the browns and kokanee salmon in the fall, and the same fishing techniques work for each.

The characteristics of large reservoirs like Trinity Lake, which are deep and have variable water levels, make them virtual deserts in terms of food supply, therefore the fish become reliant on the feeder streams to carry food to them. This requires the fish to congregate at the bocas, or mouths, of these streams. Because Trinity Lake is open to fishing all year, this trait can provide excellent year-round fishing for both fly, bait and lure anglers.

To fish these streams successfully, it helps to understand the nature of the stream and the fish's need to survive during difficult times. The most difficult periods are during summer and fall when the water temperatures are warm and the stream's ability to retain oxygen is low. Most of the spawning fish migrate downstream to the lake before this happens. Those that become trapped or don't return to the lake for one reason or another are forced to hold in the best habitat they can find. This may be a shoebox-size pool, or bathtub sized. They tend to hold right in the bubble curtain where water flows into the pool because that's where the oxygen is. That is also where food coming into the pool from upstream first appears.

Another common trait is that the stream's varying water and temperature levels don't develop the weed beds and heavy populations of aquatic insects found in spring creeks, consequently the fish tend to be very opportunistic feeders. They aren't allowed the luxury of being selective and, in fact, will go after almost anything that resembles food.

Fishing in the spring is generally tough because the streams are still high with snowmelt, and will remain high into early summer. Considering the other options available at that time of year, these streams are not necessarily good fishing choices.

But, when the runoff begins to drop, usually in May, the best fly to use is any of the ant patterns. Ants are scurrying about at this time of year and their job is to search every nook, cranny and crevice, and many of them get washed into the stream in the process.

As the temperatures begin to warm and the water levels come down, the more traditional hatches, mayfly, stonefly and caddis, will become more dominant. Keep in mind that these streams, unlike Hat Creek and Fall River, are defined more by physical characteristics than by insect populations. The fish are more interested in the presentation of the fly than in the finer qualities of the patterns.

"I like to use a size 10 or 12 black or brown Woolly Bugger with a 9-foot leader and three feet of line out past the end of the rod," says Mercier. "I can make short casts and bring the nymph right down into the face of these fish, and they'll attack it every time."

For dry patterns, Mercier uses a size 14 to 16 Elk Hair Caddis for most of his dry-fly fishing.

"Bait fishing in these streams is deadly," says Mercier. "A 10- or 12-year-old kid fishing single salmon eggs can do some real damage. Those fish have to exploit everything that comes by, and they don't have much time to eyeball it. Perhaps they do in the pools where they feel vulnerable, but the shoebox fish will definitely go for it."

Stream By Stream

This book is written with a watershed approach to the streams and the information in the previous section will, for the most part, work in any of the Trinity Alps streams.

To reach each of the streams featured here, take Highway 3 north from Weaverville.

Stuarts Fork

The first stream you'll encounter is the Stuarts Fork, which, according to Mercier, is heavily planted with rainbows. The river, as well as the other tributaries to the lake, is used as a spawning stream by ancient steelhead stocks that were landlocked by the construction of Clair Engle Dam. The descendants of these fish continue to use the Stuarts Fork and other tributaries of Trinity Lake as a spawning stream.

During spring and summer, these trout will spawn in the stream. In fall, both brown trout, kokanee salmon and smallmouth bass also spawn in the stream. Most hatchery fish are stocked at the stream's confluence with the lake. The balance are stocked either in the swimming hole at the lower end of Trinity Alps Resort, or at Bridge Camp, three miles upstream.

You can stand at the boat ramp at the Stuarts Fork, cast a spinner or a spoon, and have an excellent chance of catching fish. It's also a great place to launch a float tube.

According to Mercier, the trout feed in this area every evening. This area is also legal to fish when the stream is closed. "You will find rising trout in relatively shallow water where the lake spreads out across the flat area at the base of the stream," says Mercier. "You can use caddis, mayfly and stonefly imitations in this area. For dries, use a size 14 to 16 Elk Hair Caddis with a smoky gray or black body. These fish are not picky, they eat whatever they can, whenever they can.

"In May, right after the heavy runoff, I use a Stammet Ant which is tied with a bit of white fluff, making it easy to see, and the fish are suckers for it," says Mercier. While float tubing at the mouth of the river Mercier has had bank anglers holler at him in frustration while he's pulled in one fish after another. If you aren't rigged for fly fishing, Mercier recommends using a bubble and fly, and cast it out to the fish.

To fish the Stuarts Fork stream course, turn left onto Trinity Alps Road after crossing the bridge.

"The stream becomes wadable by mid-June," says Mercier, "and eminently wadable by July. At that time I like to fish above Trinity Alps Resort where you find surprisingly big fish in surprisingly small water. Although most of the fish are 6 to 9 inches, occasionally you will catch 14- to 16-inch fish, and I have even caught 19-inch browns in the fall and big rainbows in the summer."

This stream can be a veritable paradise for an angler. Even though a lot of people stay at Trinity Alps Resort, by and large they are not anglers. Those that do fish tend to do so where fish are planted in the swimming hole at the lower end of the resort.

From Trinity Alps Resort three miles upstream to the campground at Bridge Camp, access to the stream is very poor and this canyon is seldom fished. Mercier recommends spotting a vehicle at one end or the other, then working from the other end back to the car.

Mercier uses the Stammet Ant in the early spring, but as the stream drops, switches to a size 12 or 14 PT Nymph or AP Nymph in black, brown or orange because these colors look like caddis, mayfly and stonefly nymphs. His favorite hunting pattern is a size 10 black Woolly Bugger.

Later in the season as the water warms the fishing gets easier. "The water loses its ability to hold oxygen and the options open to the fish grow smaller," says Mercier. "They will hold right in the bubble curtain because that's the only water available in some holes. Shoebox-sized pools will hold one fish. In bathtub-sized pools the fish are spookier because there are more of them and they can see you as well as you can see them."

Bridge Camp, a Forest Service campground located at the end of the road three miles above Trinity Alps Resort, is ideal for the person who wants to camp and fish a long stretch of the stream with the convenience of a market and restaurant nearby (at Trinity Alps Resort).

The Stuarts Fork Trail above Bridge Camp enters the Trinity Alps Wilderness and parallels the stream for several miles, providing good fishing access. This is also where you encounter the side streams, Deer Creek and Van Matre Creek, where you can walk up or down the stream courses to excellent fishing that no one ever uses.

"Sometimes I fish just the side streams because these are explorations that involve more than just fishing," says Mercier. "There are more colors, a variety of grades, moss-covered rocks and old growth forests that no one ever sees from the trail.

"Even though the Stuarts Fork is one of the most popular trails in the Trinity Alps, that should not be a concern to anglers," says Mercier. "Hikers tend to be destination oriented and they will walk right past you. If you step off the trail into the stream you may not see another angler for the entire day. Most of the fishing impact is on the Alpine lakes."

One of the most fascinating aspects of the trail is its history. Following the Gold Rush there were full-sized towns with thousands of citizens along the Stuarts Fork—Opera City, which boasted the largest opera house north of San Francisco, and other communities like Saloon City. "The tread of the trail used to be a roadway and if you use your imagination you can see Conestoga wagons making their way up the road. Thousands of people used to live up there," says Mercier, "and today there's not a soul. It's wonderful."

Mule Creek

The next stream you can fish is Mule Creek. It has a nice easy trail down to the boca, about 50 yards from the highway. During late summer this area becomes a bass fishery.

Guy Covington Drive

The next significant stream is at Guy Covington Drive, which takes you to the outlet of the East Fork of the Stuarts Fork. The mouth of the stream is on a long finger of the lake, providing all-season fishing. You can launch a float tube and fish any type of dry fly in this area. There tends to be a lot of submerged trees in this area, so fishing subsurface can be a hassle.

An interesting side trip is Bowerman Barn, a historical building where you can observe 19th century construction with mortise and tenon joints, and wooden pegs instead of nails.

Swift Creek

The access to Swift Creek is Swift Creek Road, which is on the left-hand side just past the bridge that crosses the stream. This road is best known for its trailheads, including the easiest to reach Alpine lake in the Alps, Lake Eleanor, only a 10-minute walk in from the road. Lake Eleanor is a four-acre pond, which becomes little more than a lily pad pond during the summer. Eleanor is loaded with little brookies, 6- to 9-inch fish, and is a great place for a family picnic.

Another trailhead at the end of the road also leads you to the upper reaches of Swift Creek. However, in that area it's a beautiful mountain stream, and is no longer the rock rubble river course that you see at the lower end.

Upper Trinity River

East Fork-French Gulch Road crosses the stream at the head of the lake and, according to Mercier, the best fishing runs from right under the bridge several miles upstream to the confluence with Coffee Creek.

Stay on Highway 3 and take side roads in to the river.

Small boats or float tubes are the best way to fish Lewiston Lake.

East Fork Trinity River

Turn right across the bridge and drive eight miles to the East Fork. An access road on the right-hand side gives access to the stream and follows it down to the stream's confluence with the lake.

The East Fork is the first of the Trinity Alps streams to become fishable in the spring. It clears earliest because it drains from the lowest elevation. It has remarkable fishing from the road down to the lake, although few people know of this stretch. The stream flows through private property above East Fork Road and access is limited.

Coffee Creek

About four miles above the upper end of the lake on Highway 3, Coffee Creek enters the Upper Trinity from the left side. You can access this stream from Coffee Creek Road, which comes into Highway 3 just past the bridge that crosses Coffee Creek. The lower end of Coffee Creek is all private property. Once you reach the bridge at the North Fork of Coffee Creek, much of it becomes accessible because it runs through national forest.

Some tributaries of Coffee Creek are hanging streams—that is, they are cut off from the main stem of the creek by waterfalls, or rock jams and log jams. Among these is the North Fork, where a trail follows the stream into the meadows at the upper elevations.

In the upper elevations of these streams, the fish begin to look like golden trout because they've been forced to become resident fish, actually taking on the color of the streambed.

Lewiston Lake

Lewiston Lake, immediately below Trinity Dam, offers splendid trout fishing for anglers of all abilities. The lake is fed from water releases at the bottom of Trinity Dam, giving it a consistent flow of cold water. Although the flows will vary throughout the year, the level remains fairly constant, allowing the flats at the upper end of the lake to develop the characteristics of a spring creek with the same types of weed beds and insects.

Lewiston is stocked on a fairly regular basis by the DFG, primarily with hatchery rainbows, but it also receives occasional plants of brown trout and brook trout. When the fish are first stocked they are primarily the target of bait and lure anglers.

As the survivors of the hatchery fish become accustomed to the lake, they learn to depend on natural food sources which are abundant in Lewiston Lake. These fish seem to congregate throughout the upper half of the lake, among the weed beds, foraging on *Callibaetis* nymphs and emergers, which are predictable in this area. During the warmer days of summer and fall they also learn to key on the lake's population of midges, particularly in late afternoon and evening, following the *Callibaetis* hatches.

The fish seem to adapt well to Lewiston, developing the characteristics of spring creek trout, even in size, running from 13 to 20 inches in length, and even longer.

Fly Fishing

Fly fishing on Lewiston is fun. There are no worries about back casts, because you fish from the lake surface rather than from shore. Presentation is relatively easy, most anglers fish *Callibaetis* nymphs, sizes 16 to 18, suspended under an indicator.

Most of the activity is from mid-morning on, when the *Callibaetis* begin emerging from the weed beds to rise to the surface on a bubble of air. As they struggle to free themselves from the nymphal shuck, the rainbows begin moving in, feasting on this daily fare. Before the mayflies begin appearing on the surface, the fish are searching for them as nymphs among the weed beds at the bottom. As they begin rising to the surface, the fish move up in the water column, rising closer and closer to the surface as the numbers of *Callibaetis* increase.

Finally, the rainbows move along the surface, sipping the emergers out of the surface film, or taking the adults as they sit on the surface drying their wings. Sitting in a boat watching 18- to 22-inch rainbows cruise just under the surface, then slurping several emergers in a series of rises, can be intoxicating, especially for anglers who are used to nymphing in streams where they can't see the fish take the fly.

The key is to be patient, target a particular fish or pod of fish, then cast to intercept their path. Of course, the fish don't necessarily travel in a straight line, but a nymph sitting a foot or two under an indicator can be an opportunity too good to pass up for a feeding rainbow or brown.

Some anglers, like Herb Burton, don't use the indicator, preferring instead to detect the strike through feel and perception. Anglers who have the time to develop this technique will experience two to three more hookups than will indicator anglers. We recommend that someone who isn't familiar with this type of fishing either book a knowledgeable guide like Burton, or rig up with the indicator.

As the *Callibaetis* hatch falls off, the fish begin to key on the midge hatch. At this point, Burton switches to size 18 to 22 Midge Nymphs and Emergers, anticipating the next hatch event.

The midges begin coming off sometime between mid-afternoon and late evening, depending on the time of year. These can provide excellent fishing action right up until dark on some days.

The lake also has a population of kokanee salmon, although no one seems to target these fish. In late fall, the kokanee, a landlocked species of salmon, move to the mouths of the tributaries and prepare to spawn. Normally found in the deep waters of the main body of the lake, these fish become easy prey for fly anglers. As they prepare for their migration runs, the kokanee become very salmon-like, developing hooked jaws, humped backs, bright spawning colors and incredible appetites.

Using *Callibaetis* nymphs under an indicator, a fly angler can hook one fish after another until he or she tires of the sport and moves on. If you are fishing over kokanee and not having success, keep changing the leader length until you find the level the fish are holding.

Lure and Bait Fishing

Although Lewiston Lake is open all year, folks don't show up to fish it until April, when they come from as far as Arizona. Historically, Lewiston Lake was used as a dumping ground for the hatcheries in the area, particularly during the drought years when other waters were too warm for the planted fish. In 1996, Lewiston Lake received 33,000 rainbows from the Department of Fish and Game hatchery program. Whether this will continue remains up in the air as this book is being revised in the spring of 1997.

The best way to approach Lewiston Lake, whether you're a bait, lure or fly angler, is to think of it as a spring creek, not as a lake. The upper half of the lake, from Lakeview Terrace up to the base of Clair Engle Dam, is shallow, wide and, for most of the year, runs at a fairly consistent flow, not much different from Hat Creek and Fall River.

At times, however, the releases from Trinity Lake into

Lewiston are increased to pretty high levels, as high as 6,000 cfs, either for water diversion to the Sacramento River, or to simulate the natural conditions the Trinity River experienced before Clair Engle Dam was used to regulate the flows. These usually occur around the end of April and the beginning of May, and last into early June. The flows are timed to concide with the hatchery at Lewiston's release of juvenile salmon into the river. The high flows help flush the young salmon and steelhead downstream to the ocean, with a minimum of loss to predation and other factors.

During these high flows, the best way to fish Lewiston Lake, according to Jim Deichler, owner of Pine Cove Marina, is to drift night crawlers under a bobber in the upper lake, from Pine Cove up to the base of Clair Engle Dam. Concentrate on areas where the current is slower, behind the rocks and along the east shore of the lake. If you are there when the trout are spawning in March and April, Deichler recommends salmon eggs.

If you're fishing from shore, then put a single egg or small cluster of eggs with a marshmallow to float it off the bottom, especially at the mouths of the feeder streams. The fish also seem to like night crawlers. Deichler recommends putting the night crawler on with a worm threader.

The rest of the time the fish tend to hold in the weed beds, which are the generators of the lake's primary food source, the *Callibaetis* mayfly.

As the flows drop to more normal levels—from 300 cfs to 1,000 cfs—the fishing options expand to a variety of techniques.

The most consistent method for catching rainbows, says Deichler, is to troll a flasher or a dodger trailing a night crawler. Use Ford Fenders or Half Fasts with a night crawler, an egg, or a night crawler with a salmon egg on the tip of the hook. Also effective is a flasher trailing a Hot Shot or a Flatfish. The key to this is to experiment with the leader length. Trollers can use a variety of other lures, including the Flatfish or Hot Shot, fished in perch or frog patterns. Troll these very slowly.

Other lures that work well are the silver or gold floating Rapalas. Although not many people seem to use them, Panther Martins, Rooster Tails and Mepps Spinners also catch fish. Use gold blades on sunny days, silver on overcast days.

Another hot technique is to troll a Woolly Bugger or Woolly Worm in olive, black or rust. The first time I fished Lewiston I used this technique to hook and release 15 trout in two hours. Use this on days when the breeze is chopping up the water, or when rain is breaking up the surface. Tie the fly onto the end of the monofilament, and feed it out behind the boat very slowly. Troll just fast enough to keep it near the surface, even breaking the surface on occasion, but not dragging in the surface film. This setup can also be trolled with a water bubble, and even cast from shore and retrieved behind a water bubble. If the fish are hitting but not getting hooked, trim the tail of the fly so it hangs not more than an eighth of an inch beyond the end of the hook.

There are times when the trout at Lewiston take flies very well, and don't seem willing to bite on bait or lures. During these periods, put on a bubble, either a floating bubble or a water bubble

Kokanee also are plentiful in Lewiston Lake.

that will sink very slowly, tie on a *Callibaetis* nymph or midge nymph with a four-foot leader, and cast it toward rising fish. This technique can be as effective as using a fly rod.

The current in the Lakeview Terrace Resort area is slower and the water is shallower than at Pine Cove. You can often see the fish cruising the surface, looking for insects, or even while they are lying on the bottom. Although this area is better for wading, the wading is generally done from areas that are accessed by boats, usually around the islands.

Kokanee

Lewiston Lake has an abundance of kokanee, although few anglers seem to be aware of it. A few of these landlocked salmon are caught in the Pine Cove area, but most of the larger fish are caught in the main body of the lake, in 30 to 40 feet of water, in the Coopers Gulch area.

"Kokanee like night crawlers," says Deichler. "Troll a piece of night crawler behind a flasher, or use a Wedding Band, which is like a flasher with a three-foot leader and hook for the trailer."

Because these fish have soft mouths, the majority of serious kokanee fishermen rig a snubber—a piece of rubber band—between the weight and the hook.

Kokanee also take red salmon eggs, fished off the bottom with a marshmallow.

In fall when the kokanee are spawning, they will stack up in the upper lake under the docks at Pine Cove Marina, and at the mouths of the tributaries. The kokanee turn orange or red at this time of year, and look a lot like big goldfish. These fish are very hungry at this time of year and will hit almost anything. One local angler uses his fly rod, puts on a single split shot and a small piece of night crawler on the hook, casts it out in front of him and lets the bait drift down in the current. According to Deichler, he catches a lot of kokanee.

Trinity Lake

Trinity Lake is the third largest reservoir in California. It has large- and smallmouth bass, trout and kokanee.

Bass

Trinity is best noted for its excellent bass fishing and most famous for the state record smallmouth bass, nine pounds 1 ounce, caught by Weaverville resident Tim Brady in 1976. It also has an excellent black bass fishery.

Brady, who owns Brady's Sports Shop in Weaverville, says the best bass fishing on Trinity Lake is from March through May, when the bass are in one of the three spawning modes: pre-spawn, when the bass are working their way from the main body of the lake toward the coves and the shallow shorelines; spawn, when the fish are on the beds and are protecting the nests; and post-spawn, when bass that have spawned are in a heavy feeding state.

According to Brady, the bass don't all spawn at the same time. Anglers can find bass in any of the modes at almost any time during those three months.

This is the time of year when the water temperatures are right, the lake is rising, and most of the really big fish are in less than 15 feet of water.

For trophy smallmouth, Brady feels that March is the best month. "It could be feast or famine," says Brady, "but the fish caught would be big, or not at all."

"The best live baits are night crawlers," says Brady. Brady feels that fishing with crickets is not good practice because fish swallow crickets too deeply to unhook successfully, resulting in the death of undersized fish. He recommends cutting the leader rather than trying to unhook a deeply hooked fish.

"Artificials generally will outfish live bait in these months anyway," says Brady. "Use plastic worms like Green Weenies, grubs or crankbaits like crawdad or perch colored Rapalas, Fat Raps, Bombers or Rebels. The trend is now leaning toward lipless crankbaits like Rat L Traps, Shad Raps, Ratl'n Raps, or Cordell Spots.

Brady recommends sticking with one or two lures and fishing them until they work on the fish. He feels it is better to give a good lure a working chance rather than using a dozen lures and spending the day changing around.

Black bass fishing is best in the upper northern third of the lake. This end warms sooner than the rest of the lake because it is also the shallow end. It also has visible gravel beds and structure.

On the other hand, the majority of the smallmouth come from the lower two-thirds of the lake, including the Stuart Arm, says Brady.

Trout

Trout fishing is best during the cool spring months. Steve Johannson grew up on Trinity Lake and is the manager of Cedar Stock Resort and Marina. Although Steve doesn't get to fish as much as he'd like, he has a pretty good handle on what's happening with the fishing, especially in the Stuart Arm of the lake.

Johannson says the best trout fishing on Trinity Lake is in the inlets and especially across the mouths of the tributaries.

Trout gather near the tributaries for several reasons—oxygen is more abundant because the tumbling character of the streams mixes with the air, food is plentiful because aquatic and terrestrial insects are carried into the lake from upstream, and the water is cooler.

Johannson says the most consistent technique for trout fishing is to troll across the mouths of the tributaries with spinners, Panther Martins, Kastmasters, or Lucky Knights. Bait anglers can still fish by drifting or soaking night crawlers, Power Bait, crickets or salmon eggs.

Access

Trinity River (Lewiston Dam to Douglas City)

Highway 299 is the main corridor for access to the Trinity River.

Secondary accesses take off from Highway 299, such as Lewiston Road, Steel Bridge Road and Steiner Flat Road. Each area will be identified as directly accessible from Highway 299, or from one of the secondary accesses.

Lewiston Road, secondary access

Mile 0.0: Highway 299. This is the uppermost access from Highway 299, all other accesses will be in relation to the Lewiston Road Exit from Highway 299.

For access to the upper river, take the first Lewiston Exit, 28 miles west of Redding on Highway 299. This is about four miles west of the Buckhorn Summit. Turn right and follow Lewiston Road 6.4 miles, through the town of Lewiston, to the bridge that crosses the river.

Lewiston Area

Mile 0.0: Fly-Fishing-Only Section. This is the uppermost section of the main river. Instead of crossing the bridge, turn right onto Hatchery Road. The fly-fishing-only section begins 0.3 miles up Hatchery Road and extends downstream to the Old Lewiston Bridge. This area is filled with long, fast-moving shallow riffles. Migrating salmon and steelhead hold from here up to the dam and the hatchery entrance.

Mile 0.7: Old Lewiston Bridge. Cross the bridge and turn left on to Rush Creek Road. Seven-tenths of a mile downstream from the bridge is the Old Lewiston Bridge, a picturesque, one-lane bridge from the turn of the century. Next to the bridge is a fishing access, boat-launch and parking area. The river is wide and flat but holds fish during the steelhead and salmon migrations.

Old Lewiston Bridge RV Park

Rush Creek Fishing Access

Mile 2.0: There is a developed fishing access, boat launch and parking area on the left. This access is about 100 yards long and provides wading and boat access to several good pools. This is the last public access until Steel Bridge Road.

Old Lewiston Road, Goose Ranch Road

Follow Old Lewiston Road 7.8 miles to its intersection with Highway 299. Herb Burton's Trinity Alps Fly Shop is 6.6 miles down on the right. Burton runs a fly shop and guide service that specializes in the Lewiston/Trinity River area.

Mile 6.7 on Highway 299: Steel Bridge Road. Steel Bridge Road is a paved side road off Highway 299 that provides a few accesses to the river as well as a launch or pull-out access for boaters.

Mile 1.8: Day-Use Area. Turn right, follow Steel Bridge Road 1.8 miles to a day-use area next to the river.

Mile 2.2: Day-Use Area. Follow Steel Bridge Road to a flat and gravel bar area next to an old bridge foundation.

Mile 2.5: Steel Bridge Campground. Follow Steel Bridge Road 2.5 miles to the campground at the end of the road. Boats can launch or pull out here.

Mile 8.1 on Highway 299: Indian Creek. On the west side of Indian Creek, across from the Indian Creek Motel, a gravel road leads to an undeveloped area next to the river. This has several good fishing pools, and boat anglers can launch or load their boats from the gravel bar.

Mile 9.5 on Highway 299:
Steiner Flat Road/Douglas City
Mile 0.0: Steiner Flat Road and Highway 89. Cross the

bridge and turn into Douglas City, bear to the left to Steiner Flat Road.

Mile 0.6: BLM Campground. The campground entrance is on a hill 0.6 mile down the road.

Mile 1.8: Undeveloped parking area. At this undeveloped parking area next to the road the river has deep pools flowing through alder-lined banks. Getting to the river is the easy part, fishing among the alders and willows is tough for fly anglers. Spin fishermen will find it much easier. This area can be excellent salmon fishing.

Mile 2.8: Road to the river. A road to the left leads down to a flat area along the river. Another road follows the gravel bar along the river for several hundred yards.

Pavement ends. The pavement ends here. It is a good idea to stop here and turn around. A locked gate blocks the road at mile 4.5, which is not a good place to turn around.

Lewiston Lake

Follow Trinity Dam Boulevard from Hwy. 299 through Lewiston and on past the hatchery. Instead of turning left at the bridge that crosses the river, turn right, staying on Trinity Dam Boulevard.

Mary Smith Campground

One mile from the bridge you will see Lewiston Dam on the right, and an information kiosk at Mary Smith Campground, also on the right. This is a beautiful USFS campground located on the lake shore for tent campers only.

Cooper Gulch

The next lake access is Cooper Gulch, another campground located on the lake, with campsites for trailers and motor homes as well as tenters.

Lakeview Terrace Resort

Lakeview Terrace offers the only accommodations available near the lake. It is located across the road on the hillside away from the lake. Lakeview Terrace offers cabins and RV sites overlooking the lake. They also have a fleet of rental boats for their guests, and a launching facility that is available to the public. This portion of the lake is popular with fly anglers.

Pine Cove Day-Use Area and Launch Ramp

This is the only developed launch ramp on the lake. The Forest Service recently upgraded this area, expanding the parking lot and building a handicapped fishing ramp.

Pine Cove Marina

Pine Cove Marina offers boat rentals and moorage, a well-stocked tackle shop as well as boat and engine repairs. Owners Jim and Gretchen Deichler also offer up-to-date fishing information.

Trinity Lake

Take Highway 3 north from the town of Weaverville.

Mile 0.0: The intersection of Hwy. 3 and Hwy. 299.

Mile 11.7: Tannery Gulch. This is the first Trinity Lake access. It is a USFS campground with a launch ramp.

Mile 12.9: Stuarts Fork access and boat ramp. The Stuarts Fork enters Trinity Lake here. This is a picnic area and launch ramp.

The Stuarts Fork is one of the primary fishing tributaries. The Trinity Alps Road follows the stream past Trinity Alps Resort to Bridge Camp. A Forest Service road continues up the Stuarts

Fork for several miles.

Mile 13.1: Trinity Alps Road. Trinity Alps Road follows the Stuarts Fork of the Trinity River. Cross the bridge over the Stuarts Fork and turn left.

Mile 13.4: Stony Point Campground. This USFS group campground is next to Highway 3 where the Stuarts Fork enters Trinity Lake.

Mile 13.8: Stoney Creek. A USFS day-use area and swimming beach.

Mile 14.2: Pinewood Cove Resort. A private campground with camping, cabins and boat dock.

Mile15.0: Cedar Stock Road. Cedar Stock Resort is a full-service private resort and marina with cabins, houseboats, boat rentals, store and restaurant.

Mile 16.3: Minersville Road. A USFS road to Minersville boat ramp and Bushy Tail Campground.

Mile 16.8: Clark Springs. A USFS picnic area and boat ramp.

Mile 18.1: Estrellita Resort. A private marina and resort with houseboat rentals and store.

Mile 19.8: Hayward Flat Campground. A USFS campground on the lake. There is no boat launch ramp.

Mile 22.6: Guy Covington Drive. Guy Covington Drive takes you to the USFS maintained Bowerman Launch ramp and Alpine View Campground, located on Trinity Lake.

Mile 28.9: Trinity Center. The community of Trinity Center lies down this road. There is a launch ramp and a private marina. Cabins, camping, an airport and a restaurant are available in the area.

Mile 29.0: Swift Creek Bridge. Swift Creek is a major tributary that flows very near Trinity Center. It is a fast-flowing mountain stream, tumbling over a boulder-strewn riverbed.

Mile 29.2: Swift Creek Road. This follows Swift Creek upstream, offering access to the stream, and to the trailhead for Lake Eleanor.

Mile 30: Wyntoon Resort. A private resort offering cabins, motel, camping and a store. Wyntoon also has a launch ramp and boat rentals available only to their guests.

Mile 31.7: North Shore Vista Point. This is a USFS information kiosk and vista point overlooking the dredger piles at the head of Trinity Lake.

Mile 32.0: Dredger Piles. Protruding from the surface of the lake are dredger piles created by miners during the last century. These are wonderful habitat for largemouth bass.

For More Information
Herb Burton's Trinity Fly Shop
(530) 623-6757

Joe Mercier, Canyon Flyfishing
(530) 623-3306

Tim Brady's Sport Shop
(530) 623-3121

Pine Cove Marina
(530) 778-3770

Lakeview Terrace Resort
(530) 778-3803

Chapter Nine

Fall River

Jerry Vonderhae looks for a spot to anchor (and fish) on the Fall River.

Fall River best illustrates what a healthy stream can do if left on its own, without regular plants of hatchery fish and managed as a catch-and-release fishery. Although there is a two-fish, 14-inch minimum size limit from the stream's origin at Thousand Springs down to the mouth of the Tule River, killing a fish would be irreverent if not blasphemous. Too much care has gone to protect the stream and its fishery from tampering and overharvest.

The rainbows and browns in Fall River are wild, skittish and wary. Through Fall River's clear water they've seen the bottoms of hundreds of prams and canoes. They've learned from experience that a bug passing overhead that doesn't seem quite right probably isn't. The older the fish the more leader shy they become, and the more easily they are put down by a sloppy presentation.

On the other hand, the rewards of a perfect presentation with a size 18 or 20 fly on a gossamer leader initiating the rise of a 20-inch rainbow, followed by a heart-stopping run, several magnificent leaps, and finally a careful release without removing the exhausted fish from the water, are tremendously gratifying.

Fall River is arguably California's finest spring creek, emerging from the ground at Thousand Springs and then winding its way across the Fall River Valley toward the town of Fall River.

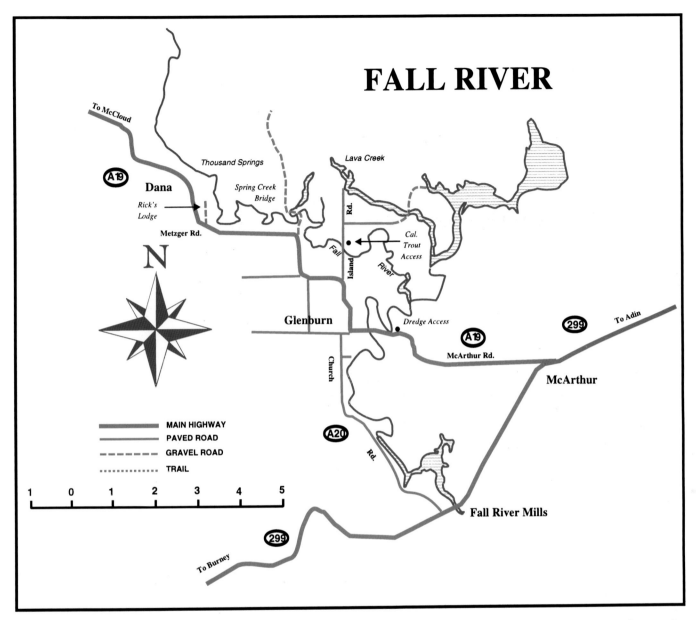

FALL RIVER

It isn't a public stream. It is surrounded by private ranchers who, for the most part, don't allow anglers to cross their land. Those that do generally charge a fee, usually in conjunction with a lodge and guide service, of which there are several now on the river.

The two truly public accesses are the Cal Trout access on Island Road, and the old PG&E dredge site near the Glenburn Church. Both have limited parking and boats must be carried to and from the water.

The stream is fished almost exclusively from boats, usually prams with electric motors, or with canoes. There are few areas that are wadable, and those are on private property. But, once your boat is on the river, you can fish the length of it, if you have the batteries, the shoulders, and the time.

Andy Burk, a fly tier from Redding with a growing reputation for innovation and excellence, guided Fall River for several years before moving to Redding and going to work for The Fly Shop. Burk's approach to fishing Fall River has been to learn about its insects, and how the trout respond to them. A serious angler intent upon becoming a good to great fly angler will benefit from Burk's approach, regardless of the stream.

Technique

The clear water of Fall River requires a finicky approach to fishing for its 18- to 20-inch average rainbows and browns. Leaders are by necessity light, 2- or 3-pound test, and long, 12 to 17 feet. Flies are presented in a downstream dead-drift known to local fly fishers as "the Fall River Drift." Anchor the boat above a pod of rising fish and select just one fish to cast to. Most of the time you will be casting a size 16 to 20 fly.

Choose a spot above the working fish where the current will carry the fly into its feeding zone, then cast so that the fly lands well above the fish and past its feeding lane. Then drag the line to straighten the leader and draw the fly in line with the feeding fish.

As the fly drifts toward the fish, pile line loosely on the water so that the fly will pass drag-free over the fish. As soon as the fly is past the feeding zone, pull it away. Do not let the fly line go over the fish, it may put them down for the rest of the day.

Burk divides the river into seasons, then analyzes the insects associated with each.

Spring

"Opening Day is probably the most unpredictable day you can have on Fall River," says Burk. "You can have bluebird weather and tremendous pale morning dun and blue-wing olive hatches, or you can have nasty weather that will knock the hatches down for a couple of weeks. I've seen times when the fishing was great from opening day on, and I've seen it so cold that you prayed for the day to end."

Mornings usually begin with the blue-wing olives, or *Baetis*, mayfly, followed by the mid-morning hatches of the pale morning dun. The hatches continue this way so long as the days aren't blustery with frigid temperatures. The best hatches occur on clear spring days, and on calm days with an overcast, although the best fishing can be on blustery days when the hatches aren't so strong and the fish have to compete for what few bugs do come off.

By mid-June, the blue-wing olives have peaked and begin to disappear, but the pale morning duns, which will peak in late May and June, and again in August, will come off almost any day that the weather is nice.

Sometimes when the morning hatch begins to slow down, Burk likes to look below the surface and watch the dozens and dozens of pale morning dun nymphs swim toward the surface. "I'll take an insect net and catch a few, then keep them in a cup in the boat, and watch the process as they become adults," says Burk. "This can give you an appreciation of what a miracle it is when, in a matter of moments, an aquatic insect transforms from a water breathing creature into a graceful, winged insect that flies away as an air breather."

As the pale morning dun (PMD) nymphs begin coming out of the weed beds to emerge, the fish's activity becomes more and more frantic as they go from a sparse morning feed, then are suddenly confronted with a huge buffet of food coming toward them. In the clear waters of Fall River you can watch the fish pick up their pace, moving side to side and up and down as their mouths open rapidly to suck in as many nymphs as they can. According to Burk you can experience some of the fastest fishing with a small HBI Nymph, an Epoxy Back PMD, or a Pheasant Tail Nymph under an indicator presented in a dead-drift downstream to the fish that are suspended over the weed beds. Those fish are waiting for every nymph that comes by.

Burk begins with his nymph five or six inches above the weeds. As the hatch progresses, he moves the nymph closer and closer to the surface because there will be more nymphs in the upper water column than in the lower. "You might have your nymph two feet or so below the surface," says Burk, "and get grab after grab, then all of a sudden your catch rate goes down. You have to be an observant angler to fish places like Fall River and Hat Creek because the changes can occur so rapidly. Suddenly, the fish will turn their attention from the nymphs to the emergers, then to the nymphs breaking through the surface film."

In addition to observing the insects, Burk is also aware of the rise forms, the visible signs of the fish feeding on or near the surface.

"When you see the rise forms change from soft little bulges where the fish are taking the insect just subsurface, then you will do well with an emerger pattern, with a nymph swung through the surface film, and you may even do well with a dry-fly.

"When you begin fishing that scenario, then you will begin to see how it all fits together," says Burk. "When fish start taking the duns regularly, you'll see the upper jaw break through the surface to suck the bug down. You will also begin to hear the fish feeding. When a fish's mouth covers the dun you'll hear popping noises as they inhale the insect, water and air. You will also see bubbles on the surface as the air is pushed out of their gills. When you see a rise form with a bubble in it, you can be guaranteed it's a clean take on the surface. If there's no bubble, it's a pretty good indication that the take was in the surface film or just under the surface."

Plenty of fishermen fish Fall River exclusively with dry-flies. Even when fish aren't rising, if a mayfly dun floats over in a dead-drift, they know it's food, it's an easy capture, so they'll come up and take it. Some insects, like the green drake or March brown, leave a heavy imprint and some fish will eat every one that they find.

Burk normally fishes until around 1 p.m., or until the hatch and the fishing slows down. After that, the river continues to get action on what he calls "garbage feeders," fish that didn't get enough to eat during the hatch so they continue to feed on anything that floats by. These can be fun to fish for, so he changes to a little Deer Hair Spider or a Humpy, which imitates a variety of insects, and continues to dead-drift them to rising fish.

After taking an afternoon break, Burk likes to come back in the evening when there can be some tremendous caddis hatches.

Summer

The *Hexagenia* Mayfly

From late June through July, and some years into August, Fall River comes alive with its best known hatch, the *Hexagenia* mayfly. The "Hex hatch" can be spectacular, beginning in the lower river and working its way upstream, sometimes as high as the Cal Trout access, although the most popular fishing area is around the PG&E Dredge Site access near the Glenburn Church.

The *Hexagenia* is the largest mayfly, up to an inch long or more, and fished with a size 2 or 4 Hex or October caddis imitation. The fly begins to hatch in the final moments of daylight and continues into the night. This can be an exciting but frustrating time to be on the river. The river boils as Fall River rainbows of every dimension throw off caution to feed on this tremendous feast.

The *Hexagenia* mayflies begin as emergers, first a few, then the numbers increase into the thousands. They rise from the surface, perform their mating dance in the night sky, then return to lay their eggs on the surface. Their egg-laying flights done, the spent duns collapse, forming a thick mat of dead insects on the river.

From the point of view of a Fall River rainbow, life couldn't get any sweeter. It's dark so they aren't concerned about predators. All a fish is required to do is swim along the surface gulping on *Hexagenias* until its belly bulges.

From the point of view of the Fall River angler, it's an exciting time to be on the river as clouds of these large mayflies swarm into the night sky, but catching a fish can be difficult during this period, simply because they have so much to choose from. The key is to try to spot a fish as it moves along the surface and place the fly in its path. An unlikely prospect as the fish are not inclined to travel in a straight line.

As darkness falls, anglers push the envelope, staying until the last moment of legal fishing time while the sounds of large trout swirling about their boat tantalize them to stay longer. As each set of headlights comes down the road one can't help but wonder if they belong to the game warden.

The Little Sister Sedge
Just before the Hex hatch comes off there is a tremendous hatch of the little sister sedge, a size 16 speckled caddis that hatches in extreme numbers just before the Hex hatch. As the pupae emerge and break through the surface film, the adults tend to run across the surface while their wings dry and, according to Burk, no fish can let that pass. During this hatch, Burk uses a small Caddis Pupa 18 to 48 inches under an indicator. Since caddis pupae are pretty active swimmers, he will sometimes cast a floating line and let it swing through the current on a tight line.

The Trico Hatch
During August, the hottest days on Fall River, the Tricos hatch. This hatch requires being on the river at 6 a.m. to catch the coolest part of the day. Burk says you don't have to bother with nymphs during the Trico hatch, because they're already on the surface by the time he gets there. The Trico hatches fade around 9 a.m., but the pale morning duns begin to kick in about then and Burk switches to an HBI Nymph, an Epoxy Back PMD or a Pheasant Tail Nymph fished under an indicator. You can get by with a size 16 in these patterns early in the season, says Burk, but as the season progresses you will have to move down to a size 18 or 20.

Fishing the Deep Pools
Although Fall River is well-known for tremendous insect hatches, it's also a great place to fish attractor streamers on sinking lines. Burk fishes the deep holes, those created by bends in the river, with a size 1, 2 or 3 density sinking line and a streamer. Burk uses a Bullethead Streamer that imitates a small trout or a squawfish fry, which can be very effective. He also uses size 8 or 10 Woolly Buggers in cinnamon or rusty brown, or leeches in the same colors. He also fishes Zonkers with a pearlescent body to imitate a small rainbow, or a gold body with an olive back to imitate chubs and squawfish fry. These are fished on a short leader not over six or eight feet long.

From an anchored boat, Burk casts toward shore, feeds out some line, then allows the current to sweep the fly through the pool. Using this technique, he can cover up to 70 feet of water with a 30-foot cast, feeding out 20 feet of line, then letting the line swing through the pool.

Fall
The fall months—late September, October and into November— kind of mirror the spring months. The PMD hatches start getting more intense, and we get the BWOs back, the small mayflies. Beginning around 7:30 or 8:00 a.m., the blue-wing olives come off, then around 10 a.m. the pale morning duns. We also get Tricos hatch through-

out the morning, and you'll find great dry-fly action throughout the afternoon.

As the fish begin to think about spawning and move upstream, streamers begin working in the deep pools and bends of the river again. Although we fish those in deeper water, they would probably work over the weed beds, too.

November can be a great month but it can also be a tough month, depending on the weather. This is the time when we have the longest days of dry-fly fishing, when the fish are already eating blue-wing olive and pale morning dun adults when we get on the river. If you want to fish dries, it's hard to beat October and November.

Access
The Dredge Site
From McArthur, take Glenburn Road four miles to the river near the Glenburn Church. The parking lot accommodates not more than 15 cars per day and boats must be carried to the river. Trailer boats are not allowed.

The Cal Trout Access
Take MacArthur Road 6.2 miles west from Fall River, turn right on Island Drive, drive 1.4 miles to the bridge. The access is past the first bridge. Parking is very limited. The access is for boat launching only. Guides and boat rentals are unavailable.

Rick's Lodge
Rick's Lodge is located on Metzger Road on the upper river. Take MacArthur Road 8.6 miles west out of the town of MacArthur. River access, boat rentals and guides are available by prior arrangement from the Fly Shop Outfitters (916) 222-3555, or Rick's Lodge (530) 336-5300.

For More Information
Andy Burk, The Fly Shop
4140 Churn Creek Road
Redding, CA 96002
(530) 222-3555

Prams with electric motors are the favorite way of fishing Fall River, one of the most productive spring creeks in California. Most of the river is bordered by private land, so there is no bank fishing and only a few public places to put-in.

Pit River

The Pit River is a difficult trout stream to wade—but wading is the only way to fish it. Here, Alan Tegethoff works a slot in his search for rainbows.

The Pit River is as good a river as any for catching large fish. Unfortunately, it is also a physically demanding stream that is hard on anglers and on equipment. But by pacing oneself and by fishing the stream thoroughly and carefully, it can be a rewarding, excellent fishing experience.

Historically, the Pit River may well have been the finest trout stream in California. Its name comes from the Pit Indians, a tribe that dug pits in the ground to trap game animals. The river begins in the Warner Mountains near Alturas and flows southwest, winding its way through the high country of Modoc's Big Valley. Reservoirs and water diversions reduce the Pit to a slow, meandering stream as it crosses the valley floor. It skirts the Fall River Valley within whistling distance of the community of Fall River, then tumbles into a narrow, steep canyon carved from basalt and lava.

The areas to fish on the Pit are those portions of the stream from the base of each dam downstream to the next powerhouse or reservoir. The reservoirs created by the dams are difficult to access, and fishing is further complicated by the restrictions on boats or float tubes.

Pit River Falls, a high waterfall, a mile or so upstream from Pit Number One Powerhouse is the upper boundary for this chapter on the Pit River.

A mile or so below the waterfall, the character of the stream changes dramatically where Fall River, roaring out of the Pit Number One Powerhouse, joins the river. Within the next few miles, the stream is joined by other waters—the combined flows of Hat Creek and the

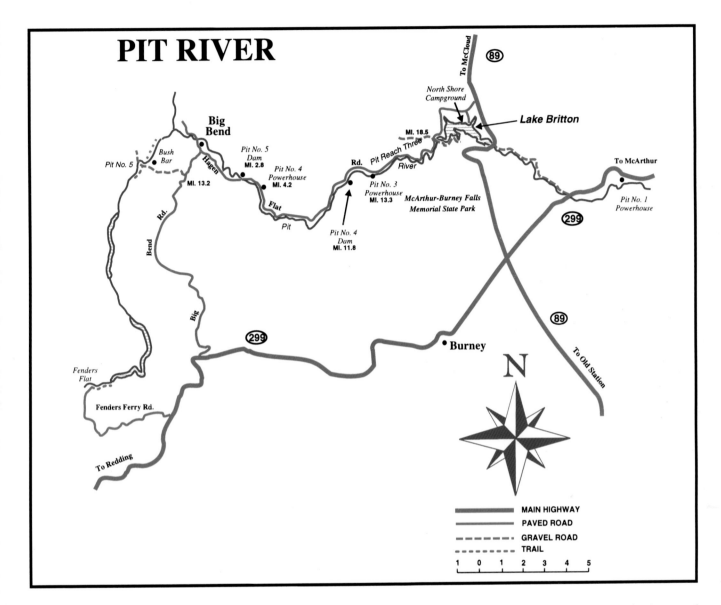

PIT RIVER

Big Bend

Bush Bar

Pit No. 5

Pit No. 5 Dam
MI. 2.8

MI. 13.2

Pit No. 4 Powerhouse
MI. 4.2

Flat

Pit

Hagen

Bend Rd.

Big

Rd.

Pit Reach Three

River

Pit No. 3 Powerhouse
MI. 13.3

Pit No. 4 Dam
MI. 11.8

McArthur-Burney Falls Memorial State Park

MI. 18.5

North Shore Campground

Lake Britton

To McCloud

To McArthur

Pit No. 1 Powerhouse

To Old Station

Burney

Fenders Flat

Fenders Ferry Rd.

To Redding

N

MAIN HIGHWAY
PAVED ROAD
GRAVEL ROAD
TRAIL

1 0 1 2 3 4 5

Rising River join the Pit at Lake Britton near the town of Burney.

Miles downstream, the McCloud River, piped through a tunnel from McCloud Reservoir to Iron Canyon Reservoir, is then released through the James Black Powerhouse into the Pit below the community of Big Bend. The Pit River finally ends in Shasta Lake, joining the Sacramento River as the largest water source of this huge reservoir, the biggest in California.

Each of the aforementioned tributaries is a major stream in its own right, but where the Pit River enters Shasta Lake it has a minimum flow of 2,700 cubic feet per second (cfs), making it the largest river in the state. The flows are made even more dramatic because power reservoirs feed each powerhouse. The flows are stored in the reservoirs when not needed, then released during the periods of peak power demands, usually during the day in the summer months.

The flow over the lowest dam on the river, Pit Dam Number Seven, located just above the high water level of Shasta Lake, runs a mere 150 cfs all night. But in the morning when Californians awake, turn on their coffee makers, TV sets and toasters, the flow suddenly accelerates to a roaring 8,000 cfs as

Powerhouse Number Seven turns on to meet the increased demand for electricity.

Pit Reach Three

This area of the Pit is notable because for 60 years it didn't have water flowing through it. When Lake Britton was built, the water was piped five miles downstream to Powerhouse Three. In 1985, when Pacific Gas and Electric reapplied for its license to operate the dam and the powerhouse, angling groups intervened and convinced the licensing agency to make water releases through this area a requirement of the licensing agreement.

As a result, gates were installed in the dam, and in 1987, after more than 60 years, water again flowed through this section of the riverbed. The rejuvenated stream responded with a great population of aquatic insets, and by providing excellent habitat for the river's population of rainbows, which quickly moved into the area. Today, this is the most popular stretch of the river.

The new stretch of water still retains the character of the Pit River. It's a tough stream to fish and very tough to wade. When I revisited the stream in the fall of 1996, I left with the conviction that if I ever went back, it would be with someone else's knees, because mine won't stand many more trips along that stream. It is no small wonder that many guides refuse to guide clients on this stream.

Technique

Until recently, few anglers fished the Pit, and many of those who did refused to return. The river is physically demanding, no doubt about it. Geologically, the Pit is a relatively young river. The shoreline and riverbed are strewn with large boulders. To make matters worse, the riverbed is covered with a leather-like slime that makes wading difficult, and even dangerous. The brush along the river is dense and in many places, impenetrable.

Fred Gordon, a guide living in Dunsmuir who fishes throughout the Pit, tells us that the anglers who do best on the stream are in their 20s and early 30s, but by changing their approach to the stream, it may be enjoyed by anyone.

Gordon says that the key to fishing the Pit is to survive long enough to enjoy it. A healthy angler who may be able to wade a mile or two of river in a normal day, would be better off fishing 100 to 200 yards on the Pit. The rigors of fishing the Pit can be overcome by fishing slowly and thoroughly, and by taking plenty of breaks.

Gordon also recommends using nothing lighter than 4X tippets for a couple of reasons: The first is that the Pit is a relatively warm stream, especially during summer, which restricts its capacity to retain oxygen. Using heavier leaders allows the angler to bring the fish in faster so that their chances of survival are better than a fish that is played out on a lighter leader. The second factor is the leather-like slime that coats the rocks. A fly that hooks into the coating will break off if tied on a 5X or lighter tippet, according to Gordon. If you tie on with 4X you will rarely lose a fly.

Wading on the Pit

Wading the Pit requires different techniques than, say, the McCloud or Sacramento River. The rocks on the Pit are large and slick, and there are bunches of razor grass along the edge of the stream. Gordon prefers not to use a wading staff. Instead, he likes to keep one hand free so he can steady himself on the rocks, even if he has to reach under water to do so. Gordon bends over, puts his hand on a rock, then works along, pivoting from rock to rock, slowly, steadily and securely.

The Pit is not a deep river, although the dark water makes it difficult to see the bottom. He recommends working out from the edge of the river to get away from the streamside foliage where casting is much easier.

Another element to consider is that you can move slower on the Pit because there are more places for fish to hold. So the key is to move slowly, use your hands to steady yourself, and cover the water thoroughly.

Spring

"The Pit can be a great dry-fly fishery in the spring," says Gordon, "especially on a rainy day." One year during high water, Gordon was walking up to the Pit with a client when he noticed a fish rise for a mayfly. Although they had rigged up with nymphs, Gordon tied on a size 12 Cahill and caught a fish on the first cast.

He and his client caught 50 fish within the next several hours fishing not more than 50 yards of stream. After moving on to another area, they caught 20 more fish, then called it a day. This was the second week of May, the river was a little high and off-

color, and the weather was terrible. In Gordon's words, "You can never tell."

Generally, however, Gordon has better luck using nymphs on the Pit, particularly with his favorite all-around fly, a size 14 Bead Head Prince Nymph fished with an indicator. (See the chapter on the Upper Sacramento for Gordon's double-fly rig.)

In spring, the Pit can follow the same hatches as those that occur on the Sacramento and on the McCloud. During the last week or two in May and the first week or so in June watch for the salmon flies (*Pteronarcys californica*) and the golden stoneflies, and be prepared with size 2 to 6 Sofa Pillows, Stimulators or Goddard Caddis'.

Because the weather at this time of year is unsettled, the hatches can occur at any time of day, and most probably will occur during late morning through early afternoon.

Summer

Gordon fishes the Pit like any stream with high temperatures and low oxygen content. He fishes nymphs in the aerated pockets and bubble curtains, using Prince Nymphs, Bird's Nests and Zug Bugs.

Fall

The *Isonychia* mayfly, a large size 8 mayfly which comes off in September, has generated a lot of interest in the Pit River. Gordon also feels that the *Isonychia* hatch offers the best chance to hook into a really nice fish on the Pit, and offers the best fishing in the region for this time of year.

The *Isonychia* mayfly emerges in midstream, swims into the shallows and crawls onto rocks along the edge of the river. After several minutes, the dun emerges as a size 8 gray-colored mayfly. During the cross-stream migrations, Gordon will cast a black Woolly Bugger or *Isonychia* pattern, size 6 to 10, across the stream and let it swing back in toward shore, or he will fish it in a dead-drift. This often results in vicious strikes, particularly among the larger fish which are attracted to the surface by this phenomenon.

Whether Gordon is using a black Woolly Bugger to imitate the nymph, or a size 6 or 8 Parachute Adams to imitate the duns, he has good reason to believe it's the size and color of the fly, not the pattern, that makes the difference. This observation has been forged by fish striking the chartreuse-colored yarn indicator on the surface while he was nymph fishing. Gordon is convinced that a size 2 Parachute Adams will work as well as any other pattern during the *Isonychia* hatch.

As the *Isonychia* hatch tails off toward the end of September, the fish no longer respond to the larger patterns. Gordon recommends dropping back to the smaller flies again—the size 16 Parachute Adams and his old standby, the size 14 Prince Nymph.

Toward late October, the October caddis become active throughout the Pit River, but Gordon stays with the nymphs— the Prince Nymph, Zug Bug, and Bird's Nest—90 percent of the time. Most of the insect activity toward the end of the season occurs from mid-morning through late afternoon because the days are colder and the water is cooler.

Access

Fender's Ferry

The turnoff to Fender's Ferry Road is well marked, just 30.4 miles east on Highway 299 from the Interstate 5 turnoff. Turn left onto Fender's Ferry Road. The pavement ends at 3.5 miles. This road becomes fairly rough but not impassable for passenger cars.

Mile 8.4: Fender's Flat. The road forks—the right-hand fork is paved, follow it .3 of a mile to a Forest Service Road 35N66. Four-tenths of a mile down a steep, bumpy road you will arrive at a flat, grassy field. This is Fender's Flat.

The road ends next to the dam. A sign warns people to stay off the dam because water levels may change without notice and sweep them from the top of the dam. Anglers can access the left side of the river by working their way along the cliffs below the dam. Access appears easier on the other side, but there is no apparent way of getting there.

The reservoir behind the dam is surrounded with a chain link fence. It is easy to understand why PG&E wants to keep anglers and others away from the reservoir. The level of the reservoir and the current speed is directly influenced by the water going through Powerhouse No. 7 upstream. Even an alert angler could be caught in a sudden increase in the water release and swept over the dam.

When Shasta Lake is full, the confluence is only a few hundred yards from the dam. When the lake is low there maybe several miles of stream to fish.

Because the water released from the dam is cold, fish from Shasta Lake congregate below the dam. In general, the water flows are so strong that fly fishing is difficult, but lures and bait work well in this area.

What is impressive is the water flow going over the dam. In spring, the flow equals that of the Klamath, the Deschutes or even the Lower Sacramento.

The left-hand fork will take you to a high steel bridge that crosses the Pit River (Mile 8.7), then winds away up Potem Creek Canyon and loops around Shasta Lake. You can view Potem Creek Falls by stopping at the first wide area in the road. A quarter-mile trail leads to a viewing area of this spectacular waterfall.

Big Bend Road: Highway 299 to Big Bend

From Interstate 5, take the Highway 299 East Exit from Redding. Do not get confused with the Highway 299 West Exit two miles to the south. You could find yourself going east on Highway 44 to Lassen Park, which may not fit your plans but will put you into some good fishing. Continue east on Highway 299 for 34.4 miles to the Hillcrest-Big Bend turnoff. Big Bend is 13 miles down a windy mountain road. The intersection of Big Bend Road and Hagen Flat Road in the community of Big Bend is ground zero.

Because the accesses to the Pit River are actually side roads off Big Bend Road, we are using the intersection of Big Bend Road and Highway 299, just east of Round Mountain, as the starting point.

Mile 7.7: Road to Pit No. 6. This road is a blind alley and ends at a locked gate before it reaches the river.

Mile 13.2: Pit No. 5. A kiosk describes the recreation areas developed by PG&E. This road crosses the Pit River and continues to Iron Canyon Reservoir. Just 1.5 miles down the road it

begins to descend sharply. There is a magnificent view of the Pit River Canyon, one of the steepest, most rugged canyons in California.

Mile 4.1: The road to Pit No. 5. Powerhouse crosses the Pit River. Here the river is a small freestone stream with large boulders. In some areas the river follows a single channel, in others it breaks up to form several small channels.

Continuing downstream leads to Pit No. 5 Powerhouse and James Black Powerhouse. A road next to the right side of the bridge leads down to the river and a large gravel bar. Fire rings mark old campsites on the gravel bar. This is a good area for bait and lure fishing. The road ends at Pit No. 5 and the gorge is extremely narrow below there. Although it is part of the reservoir, it is no more than 50 feet wide and enclosed by sheer canyon walls.

A short distance above the bridge, a road leads upstream to a paved area, the site of the old Brushy Bar School. Anglers can walk upstream or downstream from here, but the going is rough. The boulders are large—two to three feet across—which means tough walking and difficult wading. It is necessary to ford the stream several times but the fishing can be worth it. The river is open here and casting is fairly easy.

Mile 15.4: Big Bend Bridge. Big Bend Bridge crosses the river, which is fishable here and has the same large boulder character as at Pit No. 5. Nelson Creek Road winds up the left side of the river, a sign indicates that it ends 1.1 miles upriver.

Hagen Flat Road – Big Bend to Lake Britton

Hagen Flat Road intersects with Big Bend Road just inside the city limits of Big Bend. This intersection will be the starting point for the purposes of this book.

Mile 0.0: Hagen Flat Road and Big Bend Road

Mile 2.8: Pit No. 5 Dam. A nice piece of freestone stream water extends below Pit No. 5 Dam for several hundred yards before entering the reservoir. Before crossing the dam, a dirt road to the right leads to Deep Camp Campground. From the campground it is possible to work upstream along the left-hand side (looking downstream) of the river. The road crosses the bridge and continues upriver.

Mile 3.5: From here upstream to Powerhouse 4 the river flows very fast, too fast for good fishing or safety.

Mile 4.2: Pit No. 4 Powerhouse. You can access the stream above the powerhouse, but there is no path. You will have to make your way through the riparian growth as best as you can.

The road follows the river about 100 feet above the stream, it is a tough piece of water to get to but it can be done. Anyone fishing above the Pit Four Powerhouse is almost assured of not seeing another person on the stream. This is considered by some anglers to be the best area of the Pit River to fish for trophy rainbows.

Mile 10.2: The road drops back to near river level. A side road leads down to an open gravel bar that runs along the river. The river is open and easy to get to at this point. It is fairly wide and uncluttered, offering good fly fishing and spin fishing.

Mile 10.7: Another road leads to the upper end of the gravel bar.

Mile 11.0: A road drops to a flat along the river. The river is easy to fish and one could camp here.

Mile 11.5: Another road leads to the river. A sign warns of sudden rises and cautions anglers to enter the stream at their own risk.

Mile 11.8: Pit Dam Number 4. The reservoir behind the dam is about one mile long. You may fish from the bank. Boating or swimming is not allowed on the reservoir.

Mile 13.3: Pit Three Powerhouse. Water from the powerhouse flows about half a mile until it reaches the reservoir behind Dam No. 4. The water flow while the generator is running is much too high for fishing.

Mile 13.4: Pit Three Reach (below Lake Britton Dam). This area is managed as a wild trout area. The most recent regulations allowed not more than two fish, minimum length of 18 inches, to be taken by artificial lures and barbless hooks. Check current regulations before fishing.

Stream surveys indicate that the catch rate on this section of the Pit River is higher than on lower Hat Creek, although this might be influenced by the number of anglers on Hat Creek and the difficulties in accessing this stretch of the Pit River. The character of the river is a typical pool and drop stream—the river drops quickly through rock piles then enters long, slow pools.

An angler can pick his or her water in this area. There are fast-water sections where the current flows around and over large boulders. There are also slow pools where an angler can cast and retrieve small spoons and spinners, or crankbait lures such as Rapalas. The fly angler can fish mayflies in their various forms, but nymphing with Prince Nymphs is the best all-around bet. Be careful, wading is not easy.

Mile 16.2: The road climbs above the river, but once an angler hikes into the canyon walking along the river is reasonably easy. This is good, fishable water with open areas to fish from the gravel bars.

Mile 18.5: Lake Britton Dam.

Mile 19.2: The turnoff to the dam. A kiosk advises anglers of the recreational opportunities that PG&E provides. If you are coming from upstream, take the middle fork to reach the river.

Mile 21.9: North Shore Campground. This is a PG&E public campground. There is no drinking water. Offers access to Lake Britton for swimming and fishing.

Mile 22.8: Hagen Flat Road, now known as Clark Creek Road, intersects with Highway 89.

Highway 89: Clark Creek Road to Highway 299
Highway 89 passes the accesses to Lake Britton and the entrance to McArthur-Burney Falls State Park.

Mile 0.0: Highway 89 and Clark Creek Road.

Mile 2.1: Lake Britton Fishing Access. This is an improved boat ramp and parking area. Lake Britton is best noted for gangbuster crappie fishing, but it also has black bass and trout. Other species include bluegill and catfish. The trout population is a cool weather fishery that is best during the winter and early spring. During late summer heavy algae blooms cover the lake, making it unpleasant to fish.

Mile 2.4: Lake Britton Highway Bridge. A road to the left on the north end of the bridge leads to Dusty Campground and follows the lake to its upper end.

Mile 4.2: McArthur-Burney Falls State Park. This is a full-service California state campground with campsites, gift shop, store and fast-food stand.

Mile 10.9: Intersection of Highway 89 and Highway 299. Turn left onto Highway 299 to reach the upper Pit River. Turn right to go to the town of Burney and to return to Redding.

Highway 299
The Upper Pit River Pit One Powerhouse
Turn left from Highway 89 onto Highway 299, drive north past Hat Creek, over the Pit River Bridge and on up the hill. A sign on the right marks the road to Pit No. 1 Powerhouse. A recreation area for PG&E employees is on the left.

To the right is a large flat area with unimproved camping and day-use. This is an access for anglers and for whitewater recreation. This area of the Pit River does have good-sized trout but its flows are very erratic. The stream is heavily lined with willows and the stream bottom is slimy and very tough to wade.

For More Information
Fred Gordon
6283 Gillis
Dunsmuir, CA 96025
(530) 235-2673

The Fly Shop
4140 Churn Creek Rd.
Redding, CA 96002
(530) 223-2225

Truckee River

Nymphing on the wild trout section of the Truckee River just east of the town of Truckee. Nymphs are the fly of choice for this High Sierra stream.

All summer long Californians pour along Interstate 80 to Lake Tahoe and Reno to gamble, gambol and enjoy some of the most beautiful scenery in the state. Considering the popularity of the area and its easy access there is surprisingly little fishing pressure on the Truckee River.

It is doubly surprising since it harbors large fish, notably wild browns, in addition to the smaller rainbows that are stocked in some areas.

Perhaps the answer is that the Truckee River is not that easy to fish. The best parts are big, broad and move quickly through rapids and runs. It can be excellent for fly fishing but aggressive wading is necessary.

There is a 12-mile stretch of the river that is designated as a wild trout section, with artificial lures, barbless hooks and a limit on both catch and size. Currently anglers can keep two fish 15 inches and bigger. The section begins at Fish Creek near the town of Truckee and runs to Boca Bridge. Since it is ideal for fly fishing it gets more pressure than the rest of the river.

The flow of the Truckee from Lake Tahoe is controlled by a small spillway in Tahoe City. Although the river is closed to fishing for its first 1,000 feet, it is always fun to spend a few

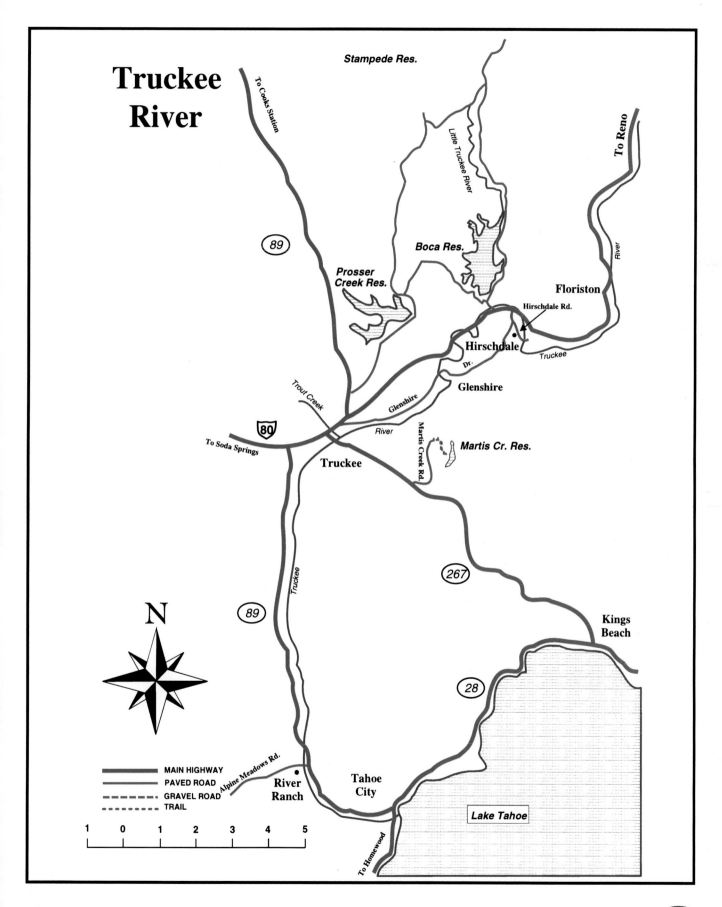

Truckee River

Stampede Res.

To Cooks Station

Little Truckee River

To Reno

89

Boca Res.

Prosser Creek Res.

River

Floriston

Hirschdale Rd.

Hirschdale

Truckee

Dr.

Glenshire

Glenshire

Trout Creek

80

River

Martis Creek Rd.

Martis Cr. Res.

To Soda Springs

Truckee

267

N

Truckee

89

Kings Beach

28

Alpine Meadows Rd.

River Ranch

Tahoe City

Lake Tahoe

To Homewood

MAIN HIGHWAY
PAVED ROAD
GRAVEL ROAD
TRAIL

1 0 1 2 3 4 5

Fishing can be good on the Little Truckee River, as this rainbow proves.

minutes on the bridge over the river just below the outlet and watch five-pound rainbows feeding.

They have the assurance of fish that know there is no danger from above as they concentrate on making the most of the constant supply of food washed into the headwaters from Lake Tahoe—or thrown in by the spectators.

The first section of the Truckee River, which runs 4.2 miles to River Ranch at the turnoff to Alpine Meadows ski resort, is mostly deep pools and fairly slow water better suited to bait and lure fishing than to flies. From River Ranch to the city of Truckee, the river is mostly riffles with a few runs and is easily accessible from Highway 89 for almost its entire length.

This 14-mile stretch of water from Tahoe City to the confluence of Donner Creek as the river enters Truckee doesn't qualify as a blue-ribbon trout stream. However, it is a great area for family fishing. There are campgrounds along the river and many more areas where a car can be parked a few steps from the water. There is even a paved bike path upstream from River Ranch.

This is a stocked section of the river and the planted rainbows can be taken on lures, bait or flies. Much of the water is open enough to allow easy casting for fly anglers and most of the year

it is low enough for wading, although the stone bottom of the stream can be tough going and a wading staff is handy to have. There are a few wild trout, mostly browns in the eight- to 10-inch range.

This is a popular rafting area when the water is high and while it is big enough to accommodate both anglers and rafters it's a good idea to keep an eye out while wading.

Randy Johnson of Johnson Tackle and Guide Service in Tahoma guides in the Truckee and Tahoe area.

"The thing about the Truckee is that you need a high expertise level to be successful. Tactics on the Truckee are no different than on the Upper Sacramento or McCloud Rivers," Johnson says.

For the 14-mile section from Tahoe City to the city of Truckee, Johnson says that during the early season there are *Baetis* hatches, some midging and a small Western green drake. There are also free-floating caddis larvae and case-dwelling caddis, along with golden stones. Nymphing is the best tactic here.

"One of the dynamite nymphs is the Gold Ribbed Hare's Ear," he notes. "In addition, I tie a marabou AP series, which is a fantastic fly for me. It is in black, brown, olive and green and is weighted, usually tied in about a size 10 through size 16. I also tie a Marabou Caddis Larva in tan, golden tan and green."

In riffles and runs Johnson suggests using caddis and little yellow stone nymphs. Caddis are good from June through the rest of the summer.

For hardware anglers, Z-Rays in the quarter-ounce size, Rooster Tails, Panther Martins in a yellow with red dots, or black with yellow dots, are effective. Johnson says that, "one lure that is effective is a Rapala CD3 to CD7 in gold and silver. Some of the locals who are religious about Rapalas take some big fish out of there with these."

When fall arrives, there is good *Baetis* fishing along with stone-fly nymphs and caddis larvae.

As the river passes through the city of Truckee, from Donner Creek to Trout Creek just east of town, it is not worth fishing. Trout Creek, which enters the river on the eastern edge of Truckee where the old logging mill is located, is where the wild trout section starts.

To get to the wild trout section, take Highway 267 from Truckee toward Interstate 80. Turn to the right on Glenshire Drive just outside town. Glenshire Drive passes above the old logging mill, where the wild trout section begins at Trout Creek, and then parallels the river for the next four miles.

The Southern Pacific Railroad tracks run between the road and the river, but there are numerous parking areas alongside the tracks. An easy walk of only a few hundred yards through the sagebrush takes anglers to the Truckee.

Since most of the land belongs to the Department of Fish and Game there is no private property to cut off access.

The first section of the wild trout water just outside Truckee is meandering and is easier water to fish that the lower, fast-water area. Fishing isn't as good here as some other areas, although there are some good pockets. Part of the problem is that the water in this area warms up as the flow drops in the summer. It also is the area most heavily fished by fly anglers.

"This is a very easy area for the novice to learn to fish," Johnson says. "It is a good dry-fly area, with good mayfly and caddis hatches most of the season and very good nymphing in the larger holes. You can also classify it as some of the best streamer water in the river—I took a 10-pound, 6-ounce brown there."

This area extends about four miles to where Glenshire Drive crosses the old Highway 40 Bridge just west of Glenshire. Upstream from the bridge is a favorite area to fish. But downstream is a three-mile stretch of the river that belongs to San Francisco Flycasters and is closed to public fishing.

The private section is well-posted. Rulings by California courts have made it possible for anglers to wade rivers and fish, so long as they do not step onto private land, but since the river is difficult to wade and the private section is patrolled, trying to fish it would be more trouble than it is worth.

After crossing the bridge, Glenshire Drive moves away from the Truckee so there is no easy access—even if somebody wanted to trespass. The private section ends at the Union Hill causeway.

Four miles beyond the bridge, Glenshire Drive intersects with Hirschdale Road, which goes to the Boca Bridge area. Glenshire Drive dead ends at an auto wrecking yard after three miles, but from where it crosses the river along an old steel bridge to the yard is good fishing. The access is not as easy as in the Truckee area—a short hike into the canyon is necessary—but nymphing is excellent. There also are whitefish in this section.

Johnson says, "It's a lot of water, this is where the river is the

biggest. There is limited wading and an angler needs to be careful. It is mostly hard, rock bottom, a freestone stream with a high pH factor.

"This is a good area because of the limited access, it takes a little hoofing. It's big-fly area—use good-sized streamers, Zonkers and big stonefly nymphs sized 4 and 6." Johnson ties a Snork-Tailed Streamer in black and in brown that represents baitfish in the system—speckled dace and Lahontan redside shiners. In this big water streamers draw big fish.

Following Hirschdale Road instead of Glenshire Drive at the intersection leads to I-80 and Boca Bridge, where the wild trout section ends.

The Boca Bridge section is an excellent area to fish.

"Upstream nymphing is the way to go and can produce 25-fish days," Johnson says. "Use short-line tactics, which offer good control. About all these areas are wadable since you can get around the larger holes."

He suggests that anglers work their way into position to cast to the prime feeding lies.

"During the early and late season there also is fantastic dry-fly activity, with caddis and little yellow stones during the summer months. There are at least 10 different mayflies on the Truckee, along with three types of caddis—microcaddis, green caddis and spotted caddis."

Johnson says flies imitating speckled dace and Lahontan redside shiners, common throughout the area, are very effective.

"Big browns really go for these," he says, noting that the Truckee is open to night fishing and most of the trophy brown trout are taken then.

Anglers who wish to stay on the wild trout section of the Truckee can backtrack by using the access to I-80 at Boca Bridge. Just follow I-80 west toward Truckee as it criss-crosses the river and take advantage of any of the several turnoffs that allow roadside parking. Don't park on the highway since it is heavily patrolled and you're sure to pick up a ticket.

Downstream from Boca Bridge is another 10 miles of the Truckee River, ending at Gray Creek, that is restricted to a two-trout limit. In the Hirschdale area there are some deep pools that are excellent for bait fishermen. Johnson says he has snorkled the pools "and there are some big trout in there. All the holes have at least a couple of five-pounders."

Rapalas are effective, Johnson says, adding that there also are some good areas for fly fishermen, who on cloudy days do very well with midges.

The three-mile stretch of deep water from Hirschdale to Floriston flattens out as it goes into the Floriston area. Although the dirt road along the river at the Floriston Exit of I-80 is blocked off it is possible to use it to walk to the river.

The Truckee is strictly a fast-water river the rest of the way to the Nevada border, following I-80 the entire distance.

From Floriston downstream a flume takes some of the water out of the river for several miles. The trout are still there but the water can be low enough to make fishing difficult.

Martis Lake

One of the most famous fly-fishing lakes in California, Martis is what Randy Johnson describes as "a classroom for stillwater fishing."

Strictly a catch-and-release, barbless artificial fly and lure area, Martis is a great float tube and pram lake.

"It has freshwater shrimp, *Callibaetis*, little yellow sallies at the creek mouths and a premier hatch of blood midges. Overall,

Martis Lake near the town of Truckee is a favorite fly-fishing spot. With lots of big fish and easy access, anglers in float tubes need to be able to match the hatch if they are to be successful.

there is a good insect structure, although there have been some problems caused by the fertilization of the golf course at Northstar."

The road to Martis is three miles southeast of the town of Truckee on Highway 267 towards Kings Beach. The "Martis Creek Reservoir" turnoff to the left is clearly marked and the paved road leads two miles to a campground that is just above the reservoir.

Easily accessible, Martis is the home of big browns and Eagle Lake strain rainbows. It's one of those lakes where knowledge is power since the right fly at the right time is an absolute necessity to be successful.

Johnson uses Martis both for classes and clients when guiding.

Early in the season he uses streamer tactics with size 4 to 10 olive Flasha Buggers, green sunfish patterns, which when retrieved aggressively draw the big browns. As the season goes on, he says, "Browns can be hunted with blood midges and *Callibaetis*. There also are small Chironomid hatches in the evening. In the summer try blood midges from early to mid-morning, either as emergers or adults. It is strictly long-leader nymphing, with 16- to 25-foot leaders. Damselflies are an important hatch cycle in Martis, which makes for some good midday fishing in June and into July. There also are a lot of

springs in the lake, so in midsummer look for spring activity and fish those areas.

"From the opening of fishing season for about the first month, use Woolly Buggers and attractors. Then *Callibaetis*, Parachute *Callibaetis* and other standard patterns, including Parachute Hare's Ears and Parachute Adams'."

Johnson recommends 3-weight rods and light tippets, either 6X or 7X.

Boca, Stampede, and Prosser Reservoirs

All three reservoirs are accessible from I-80—Prosser from Highway 89 leading north from Truckee, and Boca and Stampede from the Boca Exit of I-80.

"They can be fantastic during ice out," Randy Johnson says. "When the ice begins to break up in spring, from mid-March to mid-April, it's great to fish shallow water with nymphs, streamers and Woolly Buggers. Use sinking-line tactics."

For bait fishermen, Power Bait is effective.

Little Truckee River

An alternative for anglers is the Little Truckee River between Boca and Stampede reservoirs, a four-mile stream that can provide good fishing for browns, rainbows and, in the fall, kokanee.

The drawback is that flows are very inconsistent because of water destined for use in Nevada.

Insects are more or less the same as found on the main Truckee—caddis, *Baetis*, sulfur mayflies and dark stoneflies. In the evenings and on cloudy days there can be good dry-fly fishing with mayfly imitations but otherwise short-line nymphing is the most effective method.

The Little Truckee above Stampede Reservoir offers good early season fishing, both for resident fish and for spawning fish that have come out of the lake. Access is along Highway 89 north of Truckee and along Jackson Meadows Road. Some sections of the river are private with no access.

Hatches are the same, but ants and grasshoppers also are effective for fly-line anglers.

There currently are no special regulations on the Little Truckee.

Hare's Ear Nymph.

For More Information
Randy Johnson
Johnson Tackle and Guide Service
P.O. Box 26
Tahoma, CA 96142
(530) 525-6575

Mountain Hardware & Sports
1130 Donner Pass Rd.
Truckee, CA
(530) 587-4844

.... Chapter Twelve

North Fork Stanislaus River

The North Fork of the Stanislaus River near one of its few access points, Sourgrass Crossing.

The north fork of the Stanislaus River, stretching 65 miles from its headwaters near Lake Alpine in the Sierra Nevada to the huge reservoir backed up behind the New Melones Dam, is the centerpiece of one of California's least known and most underutilized fishing areas. Only three hours from the San Francisco Bay Area, the Stanislaus and the mountain streams that feed it are teeming with trout.

There are high mountain lakes and tumbling creeks. The river itself grows from a brook-sized trickle to a swift-moving river of rapids and deep pools. It finally ends in the

STANISLAUS RIVER

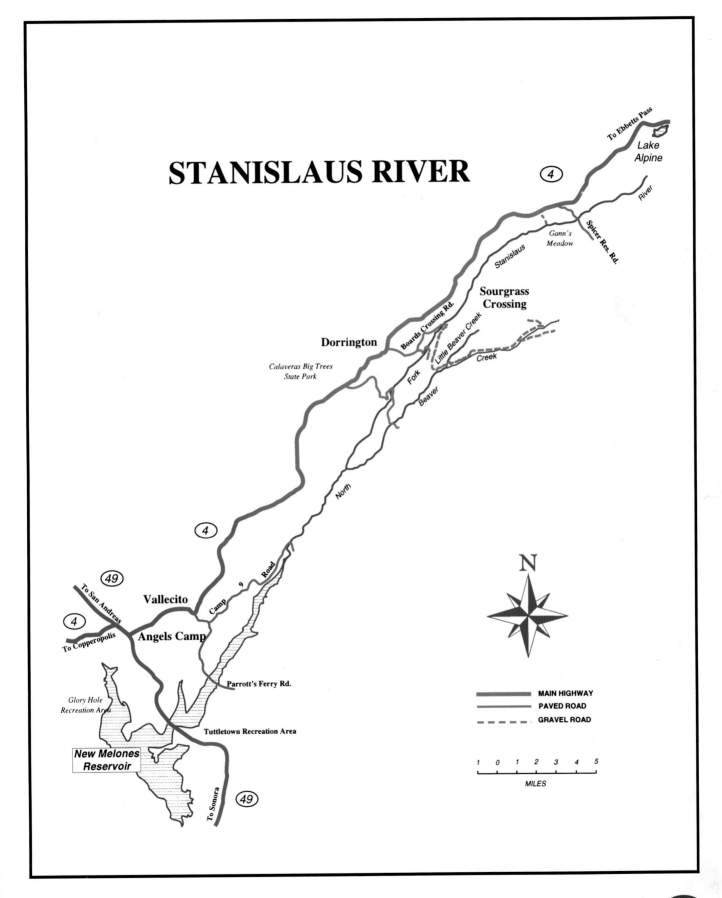

To Ebbetts Pass

Lake Alpine

④

River

Stanislaus

Spicer Res. Rd.

Gann's Meadow

Sourgrass Crossing

Dorrington

Boards Crossing Rd.

Little Beaver Creek

Creek

Calaveras Big Trees State Park

Fork

Beaver

North

④

49

To San Andreas

Vallecito

Camp 9 Road

④

To Copperopolis

Angels Camp

N

Parrott's Ferry Rd.

Glory Hole Recreation Area

Tuttletown Recreation Area

New Melones Reservoir

To Sonora

49

		MAIN HIGHWAY
		PAVED ROAD
		GRAVEL ROAD

1 0 1 2 3 4 5

MILES

23-mile-long expanse of the New Melones Reservoir, completed in 1979 after a decade-long battle between the government and environmentalists.

And all this in some of the most spectacular mountain scenery California has to offer.

Outside the New Melones Reservoir, trophy-sized trout are rare—but not unheard of—in the Stanislaus ecosystem. But the number and variety of fish make up for it. Browns, brookies and rainbows abound and almost every feeder stream or nearby lake offers fishing possibilities. Unlike many other California rivers the Stan has improved as a fishery over the past few years. Because of the New Spicer Reservoir, completed near the headwaters of the Stanislaus in 1988, it has become more of a tailwater fishery, with a controlled flow year-round that moderates the spring torrents and guarantees enough water in the dry months to keep the trout healthy and happy.

Unfortunately, even New Spicer Reservoir was unable to deal with the tremendous flow from heavy rains and melting snow in January 1997 and the floods caused mud slides that clogged the river and took out some secondary roads and the bridge at Sourgrass Crossing. Although it will take time for the river to flush out silt from the slide and return to normal (and for workers to replace Sourgrass Bridge and repair the damaged roads), fishing is not expected to be affected in the long run.

Technically, New Spicer Reservoir is fed by and empties into Highland Creek, but the creek is the main tributary to the north fork of the Stanislaus, flowing into the river just a few miles below the dam.

There are a limited number of easy-access points to the Stanislaus and some of its more popular feeder streams. These drive-up areas have paved roads, campgrounds and a constant supply of rainbows stocked by the California Department of Fish and Game. They also are the centers for put-and-take, family-style fishing. But half a mile upstream or downstream an angler often can find both wild trout and solitude. And even the easy-access areas, with some exceptions, are not crowded during weekdays.

Since the north fork of the Stanislaus runs deep in a canyon for its entire length, getting to isolated areas of the river isn't a stroll across a grassy meadow. Thanks to its years of unregulated flow, abetted by the 1997 floods, there is a tangle of downed timber, boulders and rocks that make slow-going for the angler searching for likely holes. On the other hand, that same jumble of rocks and timber offers the type of cover and variety of water that guarantees fish in just about any section of the river where you care to drop a line.

Fly fishing and bait fishing are excellent for almost the entire length of the Stanislaus, while spin fishing varies according to the area. For bait anglers, the usual smorgasbord of worms, salmon eggs, crickets and artificial baits all work well. The steady supply of planters at access areas—the DFG regularly stocks rainbows wherever it can get in with its trucks during the spring/summer season—will take about anything when they are on the bite. Wild trout, including good-sized browns lurking in deep holes, are more selective. Many local anglers prefer crickets during most of the season although Power Bait is coming on fast.

Zeroing in on the proper patterns for fly fishing the north fork of the Stanislaus is a tougher proposition since the character of the river changes as it drops from almost 7,500 feet to about 1,000 feet at New Melones Reservoir. The variety of stoneflies, caddis and mayflies may be more or less the same along the way, but due to the altitude difference hatch times vary.

Hatches are neither as prolific nor as regular as on more placid streams. The lack of fly-fishing activity on the Stanislaus has one negative—it means there is no reliable information that provides dates and types of fly hatches that are valuable in choosing patterns to tie and use. As a result, attractors such as red and yellow Humpies and Royal Wulffs are the general rule. Other effective dries include Elk Hair Caddis and Black Ants, both with and without wings, and as the summer wears on, grasshoppers.

For nymphs, Zug Bugs, PTs, Hare's Ears, Casual Dress', Peeking Caddis and various bead-heads are always popular. Still, any serious fly fisherman would do well to check what is in the gravel and on the rocks of the area being fished and to take time to identify any hatch that may come off the water.

There are no fly-fishing-only or catch-and-release sections along the north fork of the Stanislaus at this time and this is not likely to change in the foreseeable future.

Highway 4 parallels the north fork of the Stanislaus and is never more than a few miles away from the canyon all the way from Angels Camp to Lake Alpine. However, access to the river at the canyon bottom is limited, with only a few entry points along its entire length.

Specific areas and access are listed below, starting with New Melones Reservoir and working upstream.

New Melones Reservoir

The creation of the New Melones Reservoir destroyed one of the most popular whitewater sections of the Stanislaus and caused a bitter battle with conservationists, a fight so heated that one protester chained himself to a riverside rock and threatened to allow himself to be drowned as the water level rose to fill the lake.

The protest was briefly effective and for several years the reservoir was not filled to capacity. However, in the long run the government won and a stretch of whitewater that attracted 50,000 rafters and kayakers annually disappeared under the placid surface of the reservoir. New Melones was dedicated and filling began from the north, middle and south forks of the Stanislaus in 1979, 35 years after the original authorization in 1944 to build the dam.

Although the legal battles continued, including fights over whether it could be filled to its limit, New Melones was from then on a fact, although it took until 1983 to fill to capacity for the first time. At capacity, it is capable of holding 2.4 million acre feet of water, with 12,500 surface acres. Its shoreline when full is more than 100 miles.

Whitewater enthusiasts now begin their runs much higher on the river, from Sourgrass Crossing, and New Melones Reservoir has developed into an excellent fishery.

Easily accessible from the Bay Area and such Central Valley cities as Stockton, Merced and Modesto, New Melones is a major water playground. On summer weekends it is a haven for water-skiers, personal watercraft and power boaters, along with houseboats that are kept on the lake or which can be rented at the lakeside marina.

But there is enough space on the 23-mile-long lake, including numerous coves and inlets, for anglers to fish without worrying about being run over by speeding powerboaters or water-skiers. There are rainbow, German brown and Eagle Lake trout, including some trophy-sized monsters, along with largemouth bass, catfish, crappie and bluegill. Unlike most California streams and rivers, it is legal to fish 24 hours a day and there is no season—you can fish year-round.

Facilities and Access

The U.S. Bureau of Reclamation, which runs New Melones, has developed two recreation areas, the Glory Hole Recreation Area and Tuttletown Recreation Area. Both are off Highway 49 between Angels Camp and Sonora. Glory Hole is on the Angels Camp side of the lake and Tuttletown on the Sonora side. Highway 49 crosses New Melones at Stevenot Bridge.

The two recreation areas have 320 campsites available, along with boat launch ramps.

The camping areas are mostly away from the water, particularly when the lake is below its peak elevation level of 1,088 feet, and no camping is allowed outside the designated areas or on the shore. Glory Hole, a privately owned marina, has boat and houseboat rentals, gasoline, food and mooring. The only fee for Tuttletown and Glory Hole is a $14 fee for camping—entry and boat launching are free.

There also is access but few facilities at Parrott's Ferry Bridge, which can be reached by taking Parrott's Ferry Road from Vallecito, four miles east of Angels Camp on Highway 4. Turning off to the left of Parrott's Ferry Road about a mile from Vallecito is Camp Nine Road, which crosses the long arm of New Melones Lake where the north fork of the Stanislaus enters the reservoir at Camp Nine Bridge.

When the reservoir is full, Camp Nine Bridge is where the reservoir is generally considered to start and is the favorite area for a number of local trout anglers.

Fishing

For most of the year, trolling with lures is the best bet. But where the fish are found can vary, depending on the water temperature. Be advised: There are numerous 10-pounders waiting to be caught so don't undersize your tackle.

For lunkers winter is best. Trolling near the surface using minnow imitations such as Rapalas, Rebels and Broken Backs is the most effective way to find them. In late spring, the trout start to go deeper and larger lures trolled on lead-core are effective.

Overall, New Melones is rich in food for its fish, including threadfin shad and scuds. According to the DFG a one-pound rainbow planted in the spring will be three pounds by fall. For holdovers, five-pounders are common.

Fishing changes during the year and it is important for the angler to know where the thermocline is—that layer of water between the warm surface water and the colder deep water where fish are the most comfortable. Generally speaking, as the summer wears on and the sun heats the water, the thermocline gets deeper and deeper and fewer and fewer fish can be found near the surface.

A key to New Melones is the threadfin shad, which provides an abundance of food for larger trout. Unless it is an unusual year, the fish start moving to the surface in November, and until February both rainbows and browns can be found near the surface along the bank and in the coves, chasing and gorging themselves on the shad.

Inshore fishing for rainbows lasts until February, when they move to deeper water where they can be taken by trolling. In spring, the thermocline begins and slowly moves down as the heat progresses, finally getting to 80 or 90 feet by late summer, making deep trolling the only way to get fish.

Royal Wulff. Attractor patterns like the Royal Wulff are effective in fast currents where they attract the attention of fish rather than imitate specific insects.

Originally, German browns in the lake came from an unplanned plant by the DFG in 1984 when a truck carrying thousands of small browns broke down and the fish were dumped in New Melones rather than letting them die. That forced plant was so successful that the DFG now regularly stocks the reservoir with browns along with hatchery-raised rainbows.

Stanislaus River

Calaveras Big Trees State Park

The most popular area to fish, Calaveras Big Trees State Park, is three miles east of Arnold on Highway 4. A paved road makes its way the six miles from the park entrance (currently a $5 per car entrance fee) to the Stanislaus.

At the bridge crossing the river DFG stocks heavily, making it a put-and-take fishing area popular with families. For a nice weekend with the kids, this is probably the best area on the river. A 74-site campground with first-rate facilities is just inside the entrance to the park, and the setting among the huge trees is lovely. There is a second campground with 55 sites about half-way to the river, but no camping is allowed on the Stanislaus.

For a dedicated fly fisher, it might be better to go to one of the lesser-used parts of the river.

Sourgrass Crossing

Sourgrass Crossing, another popular spot on the river, is reached by following Board's Crossing Road from Dorrington, three miles east of Calaveras Big Trees on Highway 4. The paved, two-lane road winds its way down into the canyon, where a single-lane bridge crosses the river.

This area is where the 1997 slide hit, washing out the bridge and campground, along with a major new campground being built on the opposite side of the bridge. Sourgrass Bridge will be quickly replaced because of numerous government contracts with logging companies in the area, but what will happen to the campgrounds is still up in the air, although they probably will be rebuilt.

The river here is stocked with rainbows. Fishing bait near the bridge, particularly upstream, is generally productive, but pressure is so heavy during the entire season that native fish are almost non-existent. This is a good jumping-off area, with anglers working upstream or downstream to get away from stocked fish and fishing pressure.

Before the slide, fishing upstream was excellent and after the slide it should not be much affected. Every few hundred yards further along the river means that much less possibility of sharing the river with others. It also means getting away from stocked trout and looking for more wily natives, including browns that run 14 inches or better. As usual, the browns tend to inhabit deeper water and nymphs are about the only way to get them to take.

Rainbows generally are not big—most in the nine- or 10-inch range—but they'll respond to a dry-fly, particularly in the pocket water that makes up a good portion of the river. Working along the bank is not easy, which is one reason the fishing traffic dwindles quickly. There are few places where the Stanislaus is shallow enough to be waded easily until late in the season.

It is typical Sierra country, heavily wooded with large fir and pine trees. Blacktail deer are common in the area, but so are rattlesnakes, so keep your eyes open for both.

Fishing downstream from Sourgrass Crossing is easier going. Although the angler can follow the river, the first few hundred yards are unfishable rapids. It is easier to drive another quarter of a mile along the road after it crosses the bridge, park any place you can find enough room off the road, and then work your way down to the river. Several paths lead to the river and a five-minute walk will get you there. In addition to small falls and good pocket water, there also are some deep holes that the larger trout call home. But moving these big trout with bait or nymphs is difficult—they've been fished over for years and have learned their lessons well.

A trail follows the river so hiking is not as difficult as upstream. The river can be crossed during the late season when it is down, but fishing from the bank or from rocks in the river allows the angler to cover just about every stretch of water. Fly fishermen with reasonably proficient casting skills should have no problem at all.

Caddis and stoneflies are the main fare but heavy hatches are rare. Attractors, size 12 or 14, are the best all-around producers for dry-fly fishermen. For browns, size 10 or 12 Casual Dress Nymphs or beadheads can occasionally find a taker.

From Sourgrass an angler can fish all the way to Board's Crossing, about a mile downstream. Or Board's Crossing can be reached by a dirt road that leaves Board's Crossing Road (the paved road known as Board's Crossing Road actually goes to Sourgrass Crossing) just as it begins to work its way down into the canyon from Dorrington. It isn't clearly marked, but is the only other road going to the river. Although the four-mile drive down is steep on the one-lane road, four-wheel-drive is not necessary.

At the river are several houses and access to the Stanislaus is limited on either side of the bridge. However, an eighth of a mile after crossing the river there is a campground that allows easy access and is not as crowded as the one at Sourgrass Crossing.

Beaver Creek

From both Calaveras Big Trees State Park and Sourgrass Crossing there is access to a Stanislaus tributary that can provide good early-season fishing, particularly for fly anglers who want action when the season opens and the Stanislaus is too high and fast for flies.

At Big Trees Park the paved road continues for another three and a half miles after crossing the Stanislaus before it reaches Beaver Creek. There is a picnic area but no overnight camping is allowed. California DFG stocks rainbows here and at several other nearby spots on the creek. It's a great place for family fishing. Catching planters is almost guaranteed, a key ingredient for maintaining fishing interest with the youngsters. Trails follow the creek for some way so working upstream or downstream also is easy in this area.

To get to Beaver Creek by way of Sourgrass Crossing, continue along the paved road up the side of the canyon after crossing the river. At the top of the canyon, the paved road ends and the dirt road that begins there splits. To the left is the road to Rattlesnake Creek which has some nice camping spots but offers only mediocre fishing.

Following the right fork for five miles leads to Beaver Creek. It is a heavily logged area belonging to the Louisiana Pacific lumber company, which keeps it open for fishing in the summer. A gate one mile along the dirt road is locked in the off-season to prevent visitors from taking firewood out of the forest.

At Beaver Creek the road once again splits. The right fork crosses the creek and continues another 40 rugged miles to Beardsley Reservoir. The left branch parallels Beaver Creek for another five miles, allowing access at just about any point. Only a hundred yards down the road there is a pretty meadow campground set up by Louisiana Pacific with flat campsites and toilets.

Otherwise, campers can pick just about any open spot along the creek—there are plenty of them. Campfire permits generally are not required but during exceptionally dry years the rules may change, including closing the area to all visitors.

The first mile or so of Beaver Creek after the road forks is the most popular area and is stocked with rainbows. Continuing upstream leads to a more defined canyon, with riffles and pocket water where small trout abound. In spring and early summer they are eager and will readily take just about any fly offered. Size 14 or 16 Black Flying Ants are almost always a winner.

Five miles upstream, shortly after crossing a small bridge where Little Beaver Creek joins the main creek, the road forks again at a large meadow just made for camping along the stream. But best do it early in the season since most years cattle are brought into the area for summer grazing and once they arrive it is like camping or fishing in a stockyard.

Once past the meadow, the right fork of the road moves away from the creek, while after half a mile the left fork also begins to climb and easy access is lost. The left fork follows the ridge line to make a 15-mile loop and becomes the Rattlesnake Creek Road going back to the paved Sourgrass Crossing Road.

There are a lot of rainbows in Beaver Creek, feeding on caddis, stoneflies and mayflies, but most are in the six- to 10-inch range. There also are small brookies. Like the Stanislaus River, an angler can work along the creek far enough to guarantee private fishing but there is enough streamside brush so the going occasionally can be tough.

The stream, even when the spring runoff is underway, is small enough to wade with ease. The Sierra setting is lovely and unless you're looking for trophy trout it is a fun place to fish.

Ganns Meadow

There is walk-in access to the Stanislaus via a trail that can be found at Ganns Meadow on Highway 4. Ganns Meadow, about two-thirds of the way from Dorrington to Spicer Reservoir Road, is marked by several old cabins on the north side of the highway—the side opposite the trail.

Marla Tallant of Ebbetts Pass Sporting Goods in Arnold feels that the Stanislaus in the area reached by the two-mile trail into the canyon offers some of the best fly fishing on the river.

Spicer Reservoir Road

This is the last paved-road access to the north fork and has some of the best fishing. In addition, the Stanislaus is smaller at this level—5,900 feet—and can be waded by more aggressive anglers. The campground at the river, four miles from Highway 4, has toilets, water and several dozen campsites set among the tall pines.

But the game is the same—fish for planters within a few hundred yards of the crossing or make your way along the Stanislaus until you are as far from other anglers as suits your fancy. Downstream there are some deep pools, but it takes more than an hour's hiking to get to the first of them. And be prepared to wade. Once away from the campground, the best way of getting downstream is to cross from one side of the river to the other as the terrain demands.

New Spicer Reservoir

This reservoir could have been a major player in the trout fishing game but the greed of some anglers, and the unwillingness of the Department of Fish and Game to do anything about it, has guaranteed this it is just another Sierra reservoir.

When New Spicer was rebuilt to replace the much smaller original Spicer Reservoir a situation was created where resident trout tried to spawn in what became a canal from Utica Reservoir to Spicer Reservoir. The canal, named Hobart Ditch, became known as Slaughter Gulch because the big fish in their spawning mode were trapped in what once had been a creek and became prey to any angler who wanted to cart home oversized rainbows. It was a massacre for several years perpetuated by anglers (don't call them sportsmen) who cared nothing about the future.

Despite outcries from local ecologists, the DFG allowed this to continue until most of the big spawners were taken out of the lake, leaving much smaller fish and eliminating the chance for anglers to hook trophy trout under sporting conditions.

Spicer now offers mediocre fishing, with campgrounds and a boat ramp. Float-tubing along the rocky shores also is possible. In addition to planted rainbows there also are Kamloops and cuttbows—a cross between cutthroat and rainbow trout.

Lake Alpine

This spectacular High Sierra lake set at 7,350 feet alongside Highway 4 has become increasingly popular each year. With lakeside campgrounds, a store and restaurant, it's an ideal outdoor retreat. And the trout fishing can be excellent.

While a boat or float tube is best, angling from bankside can be very productive, particularly off the rocky point jutting into the lake on the highway side, or near the dam at the western end of Alpine. Bait or lures work best, particularly in the summer when an angler must go deep to find where the fish are holding.

Like most lakes, trolling is effective. During the early part of the season when the water still is cold most of the fish are shallow. But as summer heats the lake they go deeper and deeper.

If you are stuck bankside, try drop-offs, the area near the dam, or some of the coves.

For flies, the same patterns that are effective on the Stanislaus are the best when the fish are working topside. Late evening hatches occasionally have been known to excite the trout so much that the water looks like it is boiling in some places. Lucky is the angler with a boat or float tube close enough to work such a hatch.

As with lures, flies such as streamers or Woolly Buggers can be trolled with lead-core at various depths until the angler finds where the trout are holding.

For More Information
White Pines Outdoors
2182 Highway 4
Arnold, CA 95223
(209) 795-1054

Ebbetts Pass Trading Post
Arnold Plaza
925 Highway 4
Arnold, CA 95223
(209) 795-1686

Glory Hole Sports
2892 Highway 49
Angels Camp, CA 95222
(209) 736-4333

Chapter Thirteen

Carson River

Pleasant Valley Creek, three miles from the town of Markleeville, is one of the few fly-fishing-only areas in California.

The East Fork of the Carson River tumbles down the eastern slope of the Sierra Nevada, paralleling Highways 4 and 89 for more than six miles and offering numerous opportunities for roadside anglers. At Hangman's Bridge, just outside Markleeville, it turns away from the road and becomes a wild trout area.

Along Highway 89 it is mostly park and fish, with bait and lure anglers regularly catching their limit of stocked rainbows and the occasional big Lahontan cutthroat put into the river by the Department of Fish and Game after spawning on nearby Heenan Lake. On weekends and holidays particularly, such easy access leads to crowding by anglers from the nearby Nevada towns of Gardnerville and Carson City.

The wild trout section of the river that stretches 12 miles from Hangman's Bridge to the Nevada border is a different matter. Fishing is restricted to barbless lures and flies with a two-fish, 14-inch minimum limit. There is no easy access—walking or floating the river is the only way to fish it.

This section of the East Carson was designated a wild trout stream in 1986 and despite high hopes has never quite developed into the top-rate fishery that was expected. Nobody seems quite certain why, although some anglers place the blame on whitewater rafters who while drifting the river in spring and early summer take as many big trout as they want, decimating the natural brood stock.

Still, there can be good fishing available for anglers willing to work their way from the bridge downstream. There is no other way to do it since no roads go to the Carson until it leaves California. It is rugged country, but the river is large enough so that bankside walking is not all that difficult and a day-long expedition can cover several miles of water.

The area is best fished by hitting likely spots and if the fish don't respond moving quickly on to the next riffle or hole.

There's no sense working over a piece of water that may be barren since the fish here are scattered.

There is parking on either side of Hangman's Bridge and numerous signs stating current regulations. Access to the south side of the river is over a private gate (at this time the owner does not object) and the hiking here is easier than on the north bank.

Judy Warren, who guides in this area, says the favorite flies are Prince Nymphs, either with or without a bead head, a Hare's Ear Bead Head and black Woolly Buggers. For dries, try

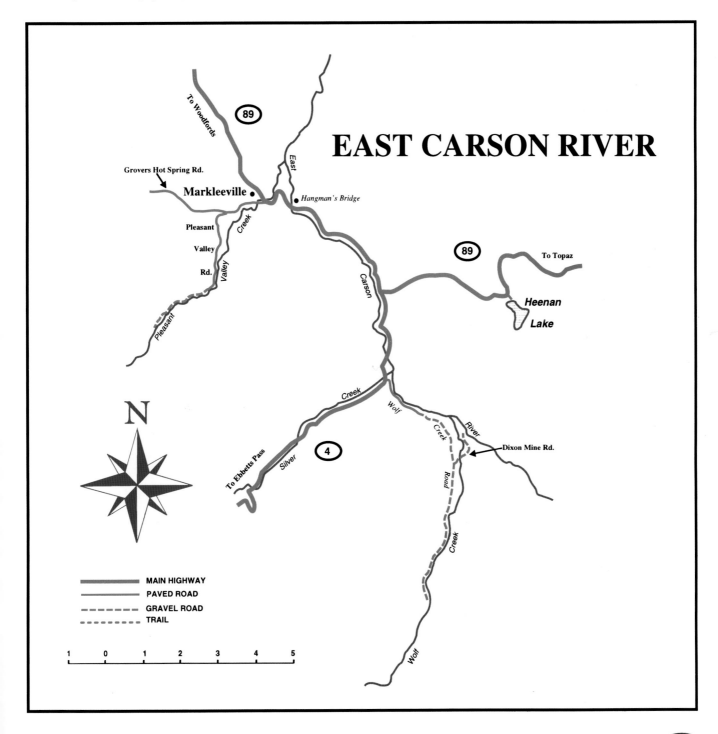

EAST CARSON RIVER

The East Carson River on the Eastern Slope of the Sierra Nevada.

down out of the mountains. For patterns, try the same as for the Carson River, but perhaps a size smaller.

Pleasant Valley

Just three miles from Markleeville is Pleasant Valley, one of the few areas in California reserved exclusively for fly fishing. It is a jewel, a pretty, open meadow that allows tangle-free casting for a steady supply of stocked fish along with wild browns and Lahontan cutthroat. To get there take the road to Grover Hot Springs State Park, which turns north from Highway 89 in the center of Markleeville.

A mile from Markleeville turn left and follow a road uphill through a housing development and on to the valley. The road is paved through the built-up area then becomes gravel for the final two miles.

Current regulations call for fly-fishing-only with a barbless hook. Anglers can keep two fish, with no special size limit.

Although there are no permanent facilities there are a number of spots that can be used for camping. The lack of facilities has caused problems for the area and fly-fishing clubs are trying to help by installing portable toilets during the summer. In addition, a streamside meadow that was used for camping (and has been trashed in the process) has been closed to vehicles by the owner to allow it to regenerate. This does not interfere with the fishing.

Pleasant Valley offers several types of trout fishing.

For the length of the three-mile-long valley, Pleasant Creek snakes back and forth within its deep-cut banks, allowing anglers to fish small riffles, slow-moving runs or a handful of deep pools where dozens of trout are often seen holding in clear water.

Although there are some bankside trees and bushes, for the most part it is open enough so that anglers don't need to worry about their back cast. It's a great place for the beginning fly fisher—plenty of fish and wide open spaces.

The road ends less than a half mile after entering the valley but the angler who wants to walk upstream can park and make his or her way through a barbed-wire gate and follow a clearly marked path. For almost half a mile the path stays within sight of the meandering creek, then cuts through a forested area for another mile and a half, not rejoining the creek until it reaches the far end of the valley. The trail is clear and level, an easy walk.

A favorite way of fishing is to follow the path until it rejoins Pleasant Valley Creek at the head of the valley then fish back to the parking area. A better part of the day can be spent doing this since for every mile of the trail the creek nearly doubles the distance as it meanders back and forth.

Another option is to fish the creek upstream from where it rejoins the trail. This leads out of the valley and into a narrow, rugged canyon featuring mostly pocket water. It's excellent fishing but can be tough going.

The third option is to fish Pleasant Valley Creek at the mouth of the valley, where the road from Markleeville enters. As the creek leaves the valley it changes from a meandering creek to tumbling rapids and pocket water. Brush closes in and casting becomes much more difficult but the payoff can be catching brown trout that are half again as big as the stocked rainbows in the meadow section.

About the only way to do it is work into position where you

any of the Adams flies—Parachute, Irresistible or standard, in sizes 14, 16 or 18—along with a White Miller. In the fall grasshoppers and Muddler Minnows work well.

Alternatives for anglers wanting to get away from roadside fishing include another stretch of the East Carson that is accessible from Wolf Creek Road, which is a clearly marked turnoff to the south from Highway 4 just as the highway and the river join seven miles southwest of Markleeville. For the first mile, Wolf Creek Road is paved and parallels the river, allowing easy access.

Then Wolf Creek Road climbs and turns to gravel, while the river stays in its canyon.

An angler can park and work upstream into the canyon as the road climbs hundreds of feet above it, or continue along Wolf Creek Road until it reaches Wolf Creek Meadows, six miles from the Highway 4 turnoff. As Wolf Creek Road drops into the meadow, a branch to the left leads past several homes and ranch buildings and across Wolf Creek to a corral before cutting steeply uphill. A sign says "Dixon Mine, two miles" but in reality the road dead-ends at the Carson River only about a mile away. It's a bumpy, rough mile but it can be done without four-wheel-drive. The road branches into several fingers just before it reaches the river, all of which end on a bluff a hundred feet above the East Carson.

There are no facilities but there is plenty of level space to camp. Numerous trails lead to the river, so access is no problem.

Just downstream, Wolf Creek enters the Carson. A number of deep holes make great holding places for bigger trout. It is possible to work downstream all the way to where Wolf Creek Road climbs and leaves the river, but it is several miles and a tough hike.

Upstream is just as good for fishing, perhaps even better. The terrain is more difficult and there is more pocket water. The fish throughout this area are wild since it's well away from the stocked sections.

Wolf Creek is stocked in the spring and generally is good fishing, although it can get too low for planting in late summer and early fall. Rather than fishing in the meadow, where cattle graze and some private land is fenced off, follow Wolf Creek Road to the upper end of the meadow, where it ends at a campground.

Working upstream provides excellent small-stream fishing and gets the angler away from stocked trout. Some surprisingly large fish can be found in the pocket water where the creek tumbles can drop a heavily weighted nymph into the pocket water below the series of small falls that mark the creek at this point.

On occasion, spawned-out Lahontan cutthroat from Heenan Lake are dumped into Pleasant Valley Creek and suddenly coming upon a couple of 20-inchers holding at the head of a pool can be disconcerting. Relatively fearless, they often stay in shallow water in plain view until an angler almost steps on them.

The other side of the coin is that there are occasions when it is almost impossible to get them to take any sort of a fly. But it's always exciting to try. A few native cutthroat also are in the creek, most of them at either end of the valley rather than in the meadow area.

Caddis and mayfly hatches are regular and any good imitation can work. Judy Warren favors mosquitoes, a black ant with a bit of red, Adams and White Millers, and for nymphs a green inchworm or Zug Bug.

Heenan Lake

Heenan Lake is eight miles east of Markleeville on Highway 89 as it leads towards Monitor Pass. The lake, reached by a short, unmarked dirt road that turns south off the highway, is 4.2 miles from the junction of Highways 89 and 4.

Covering 129 surface acres, it sits at 7,200 feet surrounded by sagebrush-dotted hills still used for summer cattle grazing. Since it was acquired in 1982 by the Wildlife Conservation Board it has been used as the only breeding area in California for Lahontan cutthroat, which are listed as a threatened species.

Heenan Lake was opened to restricted fishing in 1984 to test whether catching and releasing the fish would affect the breeding. Apparently not, it turns out, and so the limited fishing program has continued.

Regulations open the lake only on Friday, Saturday and Sunday from Labor Day through the last Sunday in October. It is barbless hook, no bait, and a strict let-'em-go policy. The entire lake is fenced and a Department of Fish and Game warden checks it regularly. It used to be that a game warden was on hand during fishing hours collecting a $3 fee, but now there is no permanent warden and the fishing is free.

Small, portable boats with electric motors can be used (gas engines are not permitted) and can be taken by auto almost to the water down a short access road from the dirt parking lot. But float tubes are the favorite means of fishing the waters, although a number of anglers do well from the bank since the cutthroat tend to hang out in three- to eight-foot water fairly close to shore.

Heenan Lake is not a garden spot—a couple of portable toilets are the main fixtures. Unless you have a fondness for sagebrush and scrub oak there's nothing special about the hilly countryside, either. Visitors make the trek for the fishing and nothing else, and the rock-strewn parking lot can get crowded when the bite is on.

And there certainly are fish. A 14-inch cutthroat is small; it takes a 20-incher for an angler to say with authority that he or she has hooked a fair-sized fish.

The Heenan Lake breeders are a full-bodied fish native to the area. According to biologists the strain comes from the prehistoric Lake Lahontan that used to cover a good portion of what is now Nevada. The remnants of Lake Lahontan today are Pyramid and Walker lakes. Due to commercial over-fishing late in the last century, Lahontan cutthroat died out in Pyramid Lake and became hybridized in most of the remaining east slope areas.

Eggs from the Heenan breeders are distributed to the Hot Creek and Mount Shasta hatcheries. In turn, the grown fish are put into a number of streams and lakes, including Pyramid, Pleasant Valley Creek and the East Carson.

For the first few years Heenan was the undiscovered hot spot, but by the early 1990s it was well-known and jammed on fall weekends—at least until the weather turned cold and windy. There have been some ecological scares, too, including a major draw-down of water by the Nevada rancher who owns the water rights and the next year an algae bloom that drained the oxygen from the lake and caused a major die-off. There were fears most of the cutthroat population had been killed but the disaster turned out to be not nearly as bad as feared and Heenan was re-opened to fishing.

There are so many Lahontan cutthroat in Heenan that on a good day it is possible to catch-and-release 10 or more fish, including a number over 20 inches. Fish from 27 to 30 inches aren't unusual. Casting or trolling small gold-colored flashing lures at a fairly slow speed works best for lure anglers, but flies are the favored means for Heenan.

It used to be that dragging a black Woolly Bugger or a small black nymph was always effective. In recent years the fish have become more sophisticated and other patterns seem to work better. Warren suggests using an Antron Caterpillar, or a shrimp or scud pattern in gray or tan. Woolly Buggers still catch fish, as do black, purple or green Matukas, but make sure to keep them a solid color with no red.

Silver Creek

Silver Creek parallels Highway 4 for almost four miles before it runs into the East Carson. A typical, tumbling Sierra stream, Silver Creek is mostly pocket water. Some of it is easy to get to when the canyon widens, but more of it is in a brush-choked gully. Highway 4 crosses the creek several times and a good way to fish it is to work from one bridge upstream or downstream to the next bridge.

Silver Creek is fishable until late in the season since unlike many other streams in the area it does not become a thin trickle during August and September.

For More Information
Sorenson's Resort
(530) 694-2203

Wolf Creek, which flows into the East Carson, is a fine High Sierra trout stream, producing mostly medium-sized wild rainbows.

Bridgeport Area

The West Walker is a pretty and accessible Eastern Slope stream, heavily stocked with rainbows.

Want to troll for trophy browns? Cast for rainbows in a fast-moving river? Fly fish in a rippling, crystal-clear creek that holds trout much bigger than have a right to be there? How about hiking? There are plenty of mountain lakes and even one so close that an easy, hour-long walk will put you among four-pound brookies.

This is the Bridgeport area of the eastern Sierra, home of the East and West Walker rivers, Twin Lakes and myriad other streams. There is so much fishing here, and so many types of fishing, that it is impossible not to find what you like.

Many businesses in Bridgeport live on fishing and the tourism it brings during the summer months. Unlike Mammoth Lakes and the Owens River Valley 35 miles to the south, it does not have a winter ski trade nor does it lose its best fishing to private ranches that charge for the right to work their streams. It is easily accessible from Southern California by following Highway 395 north or it can be reached from the Bay Area and Central Valley via Highway 108 through Sonora or Highway 120 through Yosemite Park and over Tioga Pass.

Bridgeport advertises that it has more than 35 lakes and 500 miles of streams within a 15-mile radius of the friendly little town that sits in the middle of a valley devoted mostly to cattle ranching. Many of those lakes and streams are easily accessible by paved road.

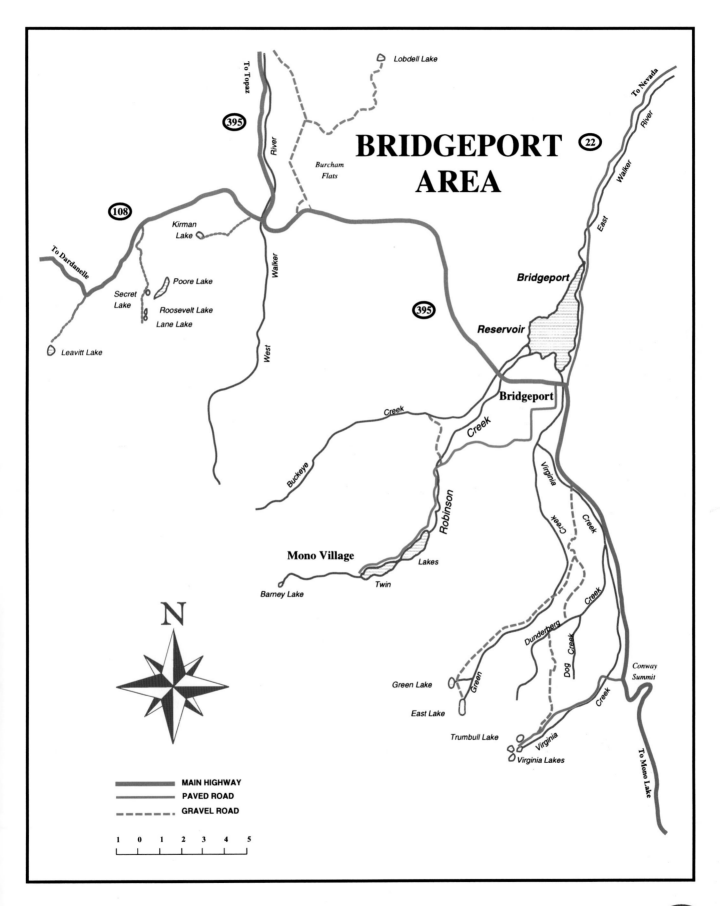

BRIDGEPORT AREA

395

To Topaz

108

22

To Nevada

Lobdell Lake

Burcham Flats

River

Kirman Lake

To Dardanelle

Poore Lake

Secret Lake

Roosevelt Lake

Lane Lake

Leavitt Lake

Walker

West

Bridgeport

Reservoir

Bridgeport

395

Creek

Creek

Buckeye

Virginia

Creek

Creek

Robinson

Mono Village

Lakes

Twin

Barney Lake

Dunderberg

Dog Creek

Conway Summit

Green Lake

Green

Creek

East Lake

Trumbull Lake

Virginia

Virginia Lakes

To Mono Lake

N

MAIN HIGHWAY

PAVED ROAD

GRAVEL ROAD

1 0 1 2 3 4 5

Campgrounds abound and family-style amenities are the rule. For anglers who like more privacy, there are numerous areas with fishing and camping that can be reached by gravel or dirt roads.

And finally, for those willing to shoulder a pack and sleeping bag along with their fishing gear, the selection of high-country streams and lakes is limited only by stamina and time.

Bridgeport Lake and the East Walker River that flows from it into Nevada are the best-known spots for fishing.

Unfortunately, Bridgeport Lake was all but drained during the 1988-89 drought to provide water to farmers and ranchers in Nevada. Little thought was given to the numerous trophy-sized fish in the East Walker, which were decimated first by the silt flushed into the river as the draw-down neared bottom and then by the lack of water.

The resulting legal action led to a court ruling that prevents this from happening again, but it took several years for the seven miles of the East Walker between the reservoir and the Nevada border to come back as a trophy trout area.

Now it is back and the fishing is excellent.

When the season opens in spring, large streamers, heavy leaders and sink-tip lines are in order. There are big fish in the East Walker and using fine leaders leaves almost no chance of landing one. So use 1X or even 0X to handle streamers tied on size 2 or 4 hooks. Patterns favored locally are black or white Marabou streamers, Woolhead Sculpins, Matukas and just about anything else that imitates minnows.

As summer approaches switch to large nymphs—Bitch Creek Nymphs are one favorite—that imitate caddis. As the water begins to drop, usually in June and July, the nymph size gets smaller, down to sizes 12 and 14. Caddis imitations and general

In October, browns move up to the base of the dam to spawn and at times it seems that every angler in California is there.

The "Big Hole" pool just below the dam is almost always jammed with anglers, and with good reason since many of the biggest fish are there. For the mile and a half downstream to the Highway 182 bridge, fly fishers wanting to wade often have to wait for enough room to cast without cutting into somebody else's territory.

Even fishing in a crowd can be both a pleasure and productive as long as streamside etiquette is followed. But occasionally bad manners on the part of some anglers make it easier to pick up and fish someplace else. Just remember, the reason this area is so crowded is because traditionally it has been the spot for the biggest fish.

Spin anglers using lures tend to do the best in the pool just below the dam, while fly-line anglers working near banks and other obstructions are more successful on the rest of the river.

The East Walker flows through private land but the ranchers allow access despite the heavy number of anglers. This courtesy should be repaid by not leaving litter.

Bridgeport Lake is a large, teardrop-shaped reservoir that holds the waters of the East Walker and several creeks. It is used to control seasonal flow to downstream ranches in Nevada. Generally shallow except near the dam at the northern end, it can be waded at the southern tip where the East Walker enters. Trophy brown trout and large rainbows are in the lake.

Rick Rockel, owner and manager of Ken's Sporting Goods on Bridgeport's main street, has lived in the area for decades. He notes that the reason for Bridgeport Lake's fast-growing trout is because it is so shallow, allowing a rich food source for the fish.

Green Creek, not far from Bridgeport, offers excellent fishing—but it has clear water with lots of brush and the trout are educated. It's one of Bill Sunderland's favorite fishing areas.

patterns such as Zug Bugs are recommended. Hopper patterns fished on top also are effective, particularly in the late summer and fall when weeds sometimes make nymphing difficult.

"All the waters that feed into it come down off the drainage from the Sierra, and that water has a chance to warm up," he says. "Bridgeport Lake is full of all sorts of aquatic foods; it has a

Lobdell Lake used to be the only place in California where anglers could catch Montana greyling. Now it is filled with Kamloops and the greyling are no longer to be found there.

tremendous minnow population, it has freshwater snails, freshwater clams and tremendous insect activity, particularly at the southern (Bridgeport) end of the lake."

Because the lake water is murky, fishing with bait or lures rather than flies is more productive. However, Rockel says that there is "the opportunity to catch some big fish float tubing in the dam area in the spring and fall, using big sculpin patterns or big leech patterns."

Otherwise, he suggests lure fishermen use Rapalas cast off the face of the dam, especially at dusk, in spring and fall. In the early part of the season trolling also is excellent, although by mid-July the algae bloom makes this method less effective. Anglers then switch to bait at the southern end of the lake where the East Walker and the three creeks that feed it come in and cut a path through the weed growth. Trolling resumes late in the season when the algae bloom is over.

Anybody fishing the Bridgeport area for the first time would be well advised to make a stop at Ken's Sporting Goods and talk with Rockel. The well-stocked store opens early and closes late during the fishing season and the constant flow of anglers in and out brings the latest information on where fishing is best and what they are biting on. Rockel is exact in his directions of how to get to specific fishing areas and what flies, lures or bait to use.

And to whet your appetite take a peek into the glass-covered freezers in front of the store, which are bound to contain some lunkers that are being kept frozen until they can be taken home by the visiting anglers who caught them.

To describe all of the fishing areas near Bridgeport would be a book in itself, but following are some of the best-known, along with a few that aren't so heavily fished. We will touch on only a

few of the many alpine lakes that can be reached by hiking, sticking mostly to the easy-access areas that can be reached by auto or with a short walk. As usual in California, what the angler makes of the fishing depends on the fisherman himself. In many places there are plenty of stocked rainbows a few steps from the car while a half-mile walk can provide a piece of the stream without company and the thrill of wild trout.

Twin Lakes

Both Upper and Lower Twin lakes are favorite family fishing areas, boasting a half dozen well-kept Forest Service campgrounds. There are stores, rental boats and other facilities along the lakes and at the privately owned Mono Village, located at the end of the 15-mile paved road from Bridgeport that leads to the lakes and then parallels their northern shore. A secondary road circles Lower Twin.

These lakes are much clearer and deeper than Bridgeport Lake—Lower Twin goes to 160 feet and Upper Twin to 120 feet. But the clarity of the water also means that these lakes do not contain the rich nutrients that provide for the fast growth of the Bridgeport trout. That doesn't mean there aren't big trout in Twin Lakes, just not as many. In fact, the state record for a brown—26 pounds, eight ounces, caught in 1987—was from Upper Twin.

Apart from the browns there is a regularly planted population of rainbow trout, along with numerous kokanee. The kokanee are small, six to 11 inches, because the plankton they normally feed on are not present in Twin Lakes. They are easy to catch, particularly in the evening when they come near the surface. Rockel says the most popular and effective lure for kokanee is the Red Magic, although a Dave Davis with a worm also works well.

Both bait and lures cast from the bank will catch rainbows, as will flies during the early mornings and late evenings. Rockel suggests using "the standard double-hook lake rig with Power Bait, Zeke's Floating Bait or Velveeta cheese fished in combination with eggs.

"Throwing lures off the bank also can be very effective. Use wobbling spoons with fluorescent colors, or a bubble and fly during the evenings. Typical patterns are Black Gnats and attractors like Royal Wulffs. We also use size 8 and 10 Olive Matukas or size 8 and 10 Hornberg Specials."

Rockel says that for trolling, which is one of the most popular ways to fish for rainbows, "My favorite is a gold-flecked, light Super Duper or a Jake's Spinner in gold with red dots on it. Other lures also work well, including the Mepps spinners, the Blue Fox spinners and small Rooster Tails either fished by themselves or with attractor blades." He urges trollers to fish in the early morning or late evening since "that's when you get the least amount of light penetration and the fish are able to come to the surface to feed."

Catching trophy browns in either of the Twin Lakes is tougher and there is little chance of hooking one except by trolling.

"The best time to fish for trophy trout is May and October," Rockel says. "The most popular proven technique for trolling in Twin Lakes is called striker action trolling. We troll at approximately six to eight miles an hour, concentrating on shoreline areas, and we use floating imitation minnow lures such as Rebels or Rapalas.

"In addition to trolling at a high rate of speed, we jig the lure, which imparts a darting action. The theory is that you only want the fish to see the lure momentarily. You want his senses to be awakened, his predatory instincts to take over so he will attack the lure."

Robinson Creek/Buckeye Creek

Robinson Creek is the outlet for Twin Lakes. It closely follows the road north to Bridgeport for nearly two miles then meanders off across the valley to end up as a feeder stream for Bridgeport Lake. It is perhaps the most popular of the family fishing areas, with five Forest Service campgrounds, including the big Robinson Creek Campground just a mile from Lower Twin Lake. There is a steady supply of stocked rainbows.

Brown trout are also in Robinson Creek but catching them is more difficult than picking up hatchery-raised rainbows. The browns are wild and have survived in heavily fished areas only because they do not readily take the bait or lures to which the planted rainbows fall prey. When they are caught it usually is by a fly fisher or an angler using a floating Rapala, Rick Rockel says.

For fly fishers, Rockel says the usual fare on Robinson Creek—and, in fact, on most of the other Bridgeport area streams—is the Royal Wulff, various caddis patterns, Yellow Humpies, and small Hornberg Specials.

The upper section of Robinson Creek is also a feeder stream for Upper Twin Lake. An angler can follow a well-marked Forest Service trail from Mono Village at the end of Upper Twin and hike to Barney Lake, about an hour and 15-minute walk upstream. Ideal for a day hike, it contains brook trout in the 8- to 12-inch range that are unsophisticated and easy to catch. Rockel suggests using worms, Power Bait, fly and bubble combinations and small, wobbling spoons and spinners on Barney Lake.

Buckeye Creek is in a drainage to the north of lower Robinson Creek after it exits Lower Twin Lake. It can be reached either by a dirt road that cuts north at Bogards Camp about 2.5 miles

north of Twin Lakes on the road to Bridgeport, or on an unimproved dirt road that heads south from the Bridgeport Ranger Station on Highway 395 west of Bridgeport. Several campgrounds on Buckeye Creek offer easy access to fishing.

The lower stretches of Buckeye are planted during the summer but by working upstream and away from the road an angler can find wild brook trout. There also are some brookies and browns in the lower stretches, along with the planted rainbows.

West Walker River

For fishing purposes the West Walker and East Walker have no relationship. The West Walker tumbles out of the Sierra alongside Highway 108 as it approaches Highway 395. It then parallels 395 north, offering easy-access fishing for a dozen miles before it spills into Antelope Valley and works its way through private land to Topaz Lake on the California-Nevada border.

As a result, most of the fishing is for planted rainbows and a few wild browns. There are several campgrounds on Highway 395 and almost the entire river is fished—and stocked—heavily. One way to avoid the crowds for a morning or afternoon of fishing is to follow the West Walker downstream from the picnic area on Highway 108 about two miles from the junction with 395. At that point the West Walker moves away from the highway and cuts northeast through a canyon to intersect with Highway 395 some two miles away. It takes several hours to fish this section of the river and it is a good way to spend a morning or afternoon. Chances of picking up wild trout, including larger browns, are much better since it is not fished nearly as heavily as the other sections of West Walker.

Rick Rockel notes that the West Walker is high in the spring due to snowmelt and during a normal year good fishing does not start until mid-June, then lasts through the summer until the season ends November 1.

"The West Walker is easy to fish, great for kids," Rockel notes. "Typical baits are cheese, worms and salmon eggs. Typical lure patterns there are smaller spinners, particularly spinners with silver blades."

For fly anglers, he suggests the same attractor patterns used on the other eastern Sierra streams, including Yellow Humpies, Royal Wulffs and Hornberg Specials.

After the West Walker enters Antelope Valley, where the towns of Walker and Coleville are located, its character changes to fit the meadowlands through which it flows. And since this meadowland is owned by ranchers and farmers access is more difficult. Once on the river, anglers can work their way up- or downstream but must stay within the high-water mark and not step onto private property.

Wading without leaving the water can be worth the trouble since the Antelope Valley portion of the West Walker is home to large brown trout. Rockel points out, however, that "it is susceptible to wild fluctuations of water level due to irrigation practices. Fishing in this area is recommended primarily for experienced fishermen using large, minnow-type lures such as Rapalas or, late in the season, hopper patterns up on top."

The West Walker feeds into Topaz Lake, which is split by the boundary between California and Nevada. Because of this, like Lake Tahoe it can be fished with either a California or Nevada fishing license.

There are plenty of rainbows in the 12- to 18-inch range in Topaz and fishing is permitted from January 1 to September 30. Both trolling and still fishing are effective in Topaz.

Rockel says, "My favorite lure is the small, floating Rainbow

Trout Rapala in a size seven or nine. We also use a lot of needle-fish in Topaz, trolling them with attractor blades with night crawlers behind them.

"Topaz is a great spring and winter fishery for the angler who wants to get out there before the other waters in the eastern Sierra are open," he says.

Kirman Lake

Although locals have known about Kirman Lake (also called Carmen Lake) for years, only this decade did it become a favorite spot for visiting anglers. It is the home of brook trout in the four- to six-pound range, along with trophy-sized Lahontan cutthroats, and is ideal for float tubing. Its growing popularity led to a change in restrictions that has helped preserve its trout population—no bait fishing allowed.

The trail to Kirman, actually a dirt road, is off Highway 108 a half mile from where it intersects Highway 395. Just across a cattle guard there is parking on both sides of Highway 108 and the trail/road can be reached by climbing a wooden stairway over a fence on the southern side. The dirt road is on private ranchland and is about a three-mile walk to the lake. A mountain bike will cut the time in half and make it easier to haul along a float tube and other gear.

The best shoreline fishing is early and late in the season—May and October—when the fish are cruising the shoreline or spawning. Otherwise, a float tube is about the only way to pick up good-sized trout.

Bill Sunderland with a Green Creek rainbow.

Rockel says that, "one of the things we know about Kirman Lake that is interesting is that the fish only live to be four years old. They have a tremendous fat buildup on their body which literally gives them heart attacks, just like humans, caused by cholesterol."

The best flies for Kirman, Rockel says, are small Olive Matukas, Spruce Matukas, small leech patterns, Zug Bugs and occasionally freshwater shrimp patterns. The basic food in the lake is shrimp, "but by fishing shrimp patterns you are competing with millions of naturals. As a result, we found that other patterns work best."

For lure fishermen, he recommends fluorescent silver spoons, including Panther Martins and Rooster Tails.

For the first few years after no-bait regulations were initiated Kirman was a first-rate fishery, producing big fish for just about anybody willing to make the short trek in. However, in the past few years it seems to go up and down—fishing can be very unproductive then suddenly turn on.

One year anglers were catching so few fish that biologists feared there had been a major die-off but when they checked they found the fish still were there—they just weren't biting.

It used to be worthwhile going in any time. Now, check with Ken's Sporting Goods to see how the fishing has been.

Highway 108

A few miles west on Highway 108 from the Kirman Lake trail is Leavitt Meadow, a jumping-off point for easy hikes to a series of

lakes that offer fine trout fishing. Just south of Leavitt Meadow Lodge is a campground with convenient roadside parking for anglers who want to walk in to Poore Lake, Lane Lake, Roosevelt Lake and Secret Lake.

All four lakes are within an hour-and-a-half walk, even less if you use a mountain bike. Poore Lake is the largest, but all offer a variety of trout.

Poore lake, like Kirman, has trophy brook trout in the four- to five-pound range and Kamloops strain rainbows that run nearly as big. The three smaller lakes have brook and Lahontan cutthroat trout that run up to a couple of pounds in size.

Rockel suggests Power Bait, cheese baits, night crawlers, worms and salmon eggs for these lakes, while the best lure patterns are "yellow-bodied spinners, particularly with silver blades, and wobbling spoons with fluorescent stripes." He suggests nymphs such as Zug Bugs or Gold Ribbed Hare's Ears for flies, along with leech patterns, which seem to work even in areas where there are no leeches.

A main food for the big brookies in Poore Lake are Lahontan redside suckers.

"To imitate them," Rockel says, "we use gold spoons with fluorescent stripes and/or streamer patterns such as a multi-colored Marabou Muddler that contains some red and some gold. The big brook trout feed on these suckers early in the morning and late in the evening when they corral them on the shallow shelves that surround the lake." He notes that the other lakes are deeper, pot-hole type lakes so those patterns are not as effective on them.

Some 10 miles up Highway 108, nearly to the Sierra crest, a four-wheel-drive road strictly for high-centered vehicles leads to Leavitt Lake. The lake has great brook trout and Kamloops fishing but at 9,500 feet it is cold and generally is iced over until late June or early July. Because it is deep, bait fishing is the best bet for anglers although occasionally flies can be effective in the early morning or late evening.

Highway 395 South

There also are a number of fishing areas on or near Highway 395 south of Bridgeport. The farthest south is a group of lakes—Little Virginia, Big Virginia and Trumbull—easily accessed by way of an eight-mile-long dirt road that turns southwest off the highway at Conway Summit.

The lakes are heavily stocked with both rainbow and brook trout and there are some wild browns. There are campgrounds both on the lakes and on Virginia Creek, which follows the road to Highway 395. Easy access means the entire area is heavily fished.

The lakes are at about 9,500 feet and normally inaccessible until early or mid-June. Some locals go up earlier when the road has been plowed and use them for ice fishing.

Bait is the most effective way to fish the lakes although bubble

West Walker in the fall.

and fly combinations or wobbling spoons also work.

Several other lakes are only a 15-minute hike away but they are not stocked and the trout generally are stunted due to lack of food.

Virginia Creek drops into a gorge as it parallels Highway 395 towards Bridgeport, but it still is accessible and can be good fishing for anybody willing to do a little hiking. The same holds true eight miles south of Bridgeport, where Dog Creek and Dunderberg Creek flow into Virginia Creek. The down timber and beaver ponds can make it tough going in spots but the reward is larger browns, along with big rainbows and brookies.

Closer to Bridgeport, after Green Creek has joined the flow, Virginia Creek becomes more accessible and is stocked. However, anglers tend to pass it by, so despite the easy access it can be a productive place to fish.

Green Creek itself is accessible by a dirt road and offers some three miles of roadside fishing. It is excellent for fly anglers and is one of Rick Rockel's favorite spots. But he warns that the clear water and educated fish can make it tough.

"Success is limited to angling skills. I recommend that high skill level fishermen concentrate on Green Creek," he says. "It is not a good place for the average family to fish because of the clarity of the water and the spookiness of the fish."

The turnoff to Green Creek is an unmarked dirt road west off Highway 395 just as it begins to drop into the Bridgeport valley.

The road forks after a mile, with a sign showing Green Creek to the left. After another mile and a

Typical West Walker hatchery rainbow.

half, the road forks again with a hard, uphill turn to the right leading to Green Creek. From where the road joins Green Creek at a pond known as the Gauging Station it parallels the creek, which is shaded by aspen and other trees and brush. There also is a meadow where the creek has been slowed by beaver ponds. The beaver ponds are tough fishing because every step creates movement that scares the fish, but making the effort can be rewarding.

Rockel says that, "patterns I like to fish on Green Creek are

Black Flying Ants in size 16, attractor patterns like a Royal Wulff or Yellow Humpy, size 16, or caddis or mayfly patterns in sizes 14 and 16. Typically, the caddis patterns have an olive thorax and the mayflies are cream-colored, such as the Light Cahill or Pale Morning Dun."

At the end of the road is a campground, which also is the trailhead for three popular lakes—Green Lake, East Lake and West Lake. They all contain rainbows, browns and brookies, some of them quite large. East Lake and Green Lake are the most popular, with good bait fishing or lure fishing throughout the summer.

In October, West Lake is noted for 16- to 20-inch brown trout, usually taken on large, gold wobbling spoons. Smaller fish are available in all three lakes throughout the season and Rockel says they'll bite "on any technique you like."

Lobdell Lake

Fourteen miles north of Bridgeport on Highway 395 is a turnoff to the east marked "Burcham Flats/Lobdell Lake." About four miles along the road a branch to the right eventually leads to Lobdell Lake, a man-made reservoir that turns into little more than a large mud puddle late in the season.

Lobdell is mentioned only because of what it had until the mid-1990s—a thriving population of Montana greyling. It was the only place you could catch them in California. However, there was a sudden winter die-off for unexplained reasons. DFG biologists have investigated but don't know what happened. Since then, kokanee have been planted and thrive in Lobdell, drawing almost as many anglers as when there were greyling.

For More Information
Rick Rockel
Ken's Sporting Goods
Main Street
Bridgeport, CA 93517
(760) 932-7707

Owens River

The Owens River near the town of Mammoth Lakes is a large spring creek with one of the highest trout populations in California—11,000 trout to the mile. It's tough fishing with clear water and huge rainbows and browns. Here Bill Sunderland works a slot on the barren-banked river.

"The eastern slope of the Sierra," I've been told for years, "has more and bigger trout than anyplace else in California." There's an easy way to prove it—fish the Owens River Valley area near Mammoth Lakes. Both the Owens River and Hot Creek are nutrient-rich spring creeks that hold an amazing number of big fish. And they empty into Crowley Lake, which is noted for its trophy trout.

A California Department of Fish and Game electroshock survey of both streams found more than 11,000 fish per mile in each of them. At Hot Creek, they turned up 10,018 browns and 1,396 rainbows per mile, for a total of 11,414 fish. For the Owens River, it was 2,262 browns and 8,785 rainbows for a total of 11,047. The fish came in all sizes, but with plenty of big ones.

That's the good news. The bad news is that there isn't much of either stream open to public access. What is fishable for free is mostly limited to barbless fly or lure fishing with size and limit restrictions.

Much of both streams is in private hands—two fishing ranches and a private ranch on the Owens and one fishing resort on Hot Creek. They allow only guests who stay there to fish their section of the water.

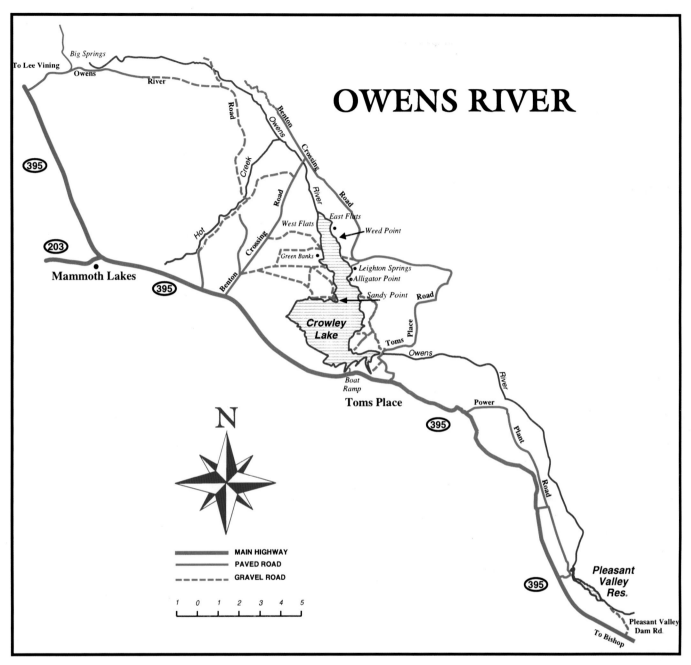

On the Owens above Crowley Lake are Alper's Owens River Ranch and Arcularius Ranch, while on Hot Creek there is Hot Creek Ranch. All three are heavily booked in advance and all three have restrictions on their fishing. Alper's Owens River Ranch and Arcularius Ranch allow fly-fishing-only and it is all barbless hook, catch-and-release. Hot Creek Ranch is the same with an added caveat, dry-flies only. When the ranch was sold years back it was with a clause that only dry-fly fishing would be allowed on its waters. That can be frustrating when guests can see 20-inch browns nymphing on the bottom and can't move them up top to take dries. But nobody ever said fly fishing was supposed to be easy.

Trout in both the Owens and Hot Creek are mostly wild. Stocking occurs in public areas only in midsummer when the big trout from Crowley Lake are not in the streams to spawn.

Hot Creek runs into the Owens River, which in turn feeds Crowley Lake, a large reservoir that sends its water downstream to Los Angeles. There also is good fishing on the Owens below Crowley and much of it doesn't carry the restrictions that exist above the reservoir. On the other hand, it doesn't have so many trophy fish, either.

The Mammoth Lakes area, part of the Inyo National Forest, is a rich fishery with numerous lakes and streams. Many of them are stocked and anglers who prefer to use bait or like to eat their catch can fish just about any type of water they want. There's a good variety of camping and hiking along with spectacular scenery.

The Owens River Valley, which runs through the middle of the national forest, is 7,000 feet high and is roughly the same distance from Los Angeles as it is from San Francisco.

Upper Owens River

The headwaters of the Owens are at Big Springs, just two miles off Highway 395 along Owens River Road. Owens River Road is a clearly marked turnoff to the east seven miles north of Mammoth Lakes. Big Springs is a public campsite and fishing is open to the public for about a mile downstream until it hits Alper's Owens River Ranch. Regulations are two fish, 16 inches or larger, barbless lures or flies.

(Note: Always check regulations since they can change year by year. Where special regulations exist at the time of writing they are mentioned so anglers not interested in that type of fishing won't be surprised to find such restrictions when they get there.)

It is only about a dozen air miles from Big Springs to Crowley, but the Owens is a meandering meadow stream that with all its loops and twists covers close to 30 miles. Throughout the fishing season it is clear and clean, even though there is some snowmelt in the spring. Its water level varies little and the smorgasbord of caddis, stoneflies, mayflies and midges allow trout to grow quickly to trophy size.

It is a typical example of an excellent spring creek and the same abundance of food and clear water that allow trout growth also make it demanding fishing. Owens River trout see plenty of artificials and have the time to inspect an angler's offerings before taking—or refusing—them. As a result, long leaders, pinpoint casts with drag-free drifts and match-the-hatch flies are a must.

Another difficulty is the wind. Although it tends to drop in late afternoon and evening, there are days when there is no letup and tangled leaders and wind knots are the norm for everybody but the expert caster.

Finally, most of the surrounding countryside is open with no bank-side trees or brush to screen the angler, so creeping on hands and knees to get into position to cast to spooky trout can pay off. Remember, if you can see them then they can see you, so the less of yourself that shows above the bank the better chance you have of catching a lunker rather than simply saying good-bye as it torpedoes downstream.

There's less than a mile of public access from Big Springs to the Alper's Owens River Ranch. The ranch has about two miles of stream, along with a man-made float-tube pond stocked with lunkers, and borders on the Arcularius Ranch, which owns almost five miles of Owens River bankside. It was on Arcularius Ranch where the DFG shocked the stream to measure the trout population.

The ranch, owned and run by the Arcularius family since it became a fishing ranch in 1919 (although it is up for sale), has fewer than 20 cabins. Most of the cabins are large, with two or three bedrooms, and are fine for a group of anglers. Even at capacity there's enough room on the ranch to comfortably fish a stretch of the stream without feeling crowded. The entire river has easy access, allowing anglers to drive their cars to whatever spot they like.

The ranch continues to run more than 100 head of cattle, including several bulls, and although they feed along the river they have not broken down the banks as has been done to some other creeks where cattle run free. It can be disconcerting to look over your shoulder and see a bull behind you but it quickly becomes obvious that they are used to seeing people.

Downstream, there is another ranch, which is closed to the public. But below that the Owens River is open to fishing downstream to where it feeds into Crowley. It is about five miles as the crow flies but double that walking the stream bank.

There are two ways to get to the public section of the Owens.

The first is to follow Owens River Road for more than five miles past the various ranches. Just past a cattle gate is a dirt road to the left that goes to the river in what is known as the Long Ears section. A second way is via Benton Crossing, a paved road that can be reached from Highway 395 just south of the turnoff to Mammoth Lakes. It crosses the Owens about a mile upstream from where it enters Crowley.

The Owens River from Big Springs to Crowley, whether on public or private land, is fished the same way. The stream, the fish and the insects are the same and trout are everywhere.

The Owens is a migratory hatchery with rainbows coming upriver to spawn in spring and the big browns moving up from Crowley in fall. Although there are plenty of big resident fish in the river in between, those are the periods when the biggest fish are caught.

Caddis are a major food on the Owens and the flies should match them. Just about any caddis pattern works, but the ubiquitous Elk Hair Caddis size 12 to 16 is a perennial favorite. A CDC Caddis Emerger also is very effective, while for nymphs try Gold Ribbed Hare's Ears size 12 or 14, Bead-Head PTs and Bird's Nests, size 12 or 14, and olive or orange scuds.

Streamers attract big trout, so don't forget to bring along a selection of Woolly Buggers, Matukas and Clouser Minnows, sizes 6 and 8.

When the season opens in late April, the Owens is basically a nymph fishery, but within weeks anglers can switch to dries and score on the big fish by using the classic Fall River drift technique, with long leaders and absolutely no drag.

After spawning, along about the middle or end of May, the big fish start moving downstream again to return to Crowley. It's then that the fishing picks up on the private ranches, or in the public stretch from below the ranches to Crowley Lake.

Fred Rowe, a guide who has fished the area for years, says, "There are two ways to fish during this period—you either have to get flies down deep and into the holes, or you can strip them in and out of the cut banks and get the fish to come out and take them. The problem with fishing this section of the river is that it is real hit or miss because you have to find the fish. They are not podded up, so the trick is to cover a lot of territory to find one or two big fish.

"You cast and you cover the water, get the flies down deep. If you don't get anything, keep going. Cast and move, cast and move."

By the Fourth of July most big fish have returned to Crowley and although the action on dries becomes fast and furious on the Owens most of the fish are smaller. In October, when the browns and rainbows again are spawning, they come out of Crowley and begin to work their way upriver. Yes, rainbows—there is a fall-breeding strain in Crowley along with the more normal spring spawners.

As the fish move onto the ranches, and if an angler hasn't booked the year before, it is tough finding room during this period. The spawners eventually will hit Big Springs once again as the season draws to a close. But remember, it's about 7,000 feet in elevation and can get cold, with snow flurries not unheard of.

The stretch of river from the ranches to Crowley has become more popular in recent years and in November 1996 a fence to keep cattle from trampling the bank was completed, which should make it even better fishing as time goes on, and the undercut banks provide more and more spots for trout to hold. The regulations on this section of the river, from the private ranches to Benton Crossing Bridge, are artificial flies and lures, barbless hooks and a two-trout limit of 16 inches or less.

From Benton Crossing downstream to the fishing monument, which is about one-quarter of a mile upstream from the maximum lake level, there are no special restrictions. From the monument to Crowley Lake there are no special restrictions until August 1. From then until the end of the season it is artificial lures, barbless hooks and an 18-inch minimum for the two trout anglers are allowed to keep.

Hot Creek

The best way to start fishing Hot Creek is to stop by the Hot Creek Hatchery just off Highway 395 and take a look at the thousands of 20-inch (and larger!) trout in the holding pens. That way you won't feel so overwhelmed the first time you spot three or four rainbows that size holding in the creek.

There isn't much of Hot Creek to fish but what there is can be tremendous. This isn't exactly a secret so fishing there without company is a rarity.

Just below the hatchery is a short stretch of Hot Creek that is open to the public but was not well-known for years. Now it is popular, with what appears at times to be almost as many anglers as fish. To get to this few hundreds yards of Hot Creek take an unmarked dirt road that turns off Hot Creek hatchery road just beyond the turnoff to the hatchery. If you go to the turnoff to Hot Creek Ranch you've gone too far.

Below this section a bit more than two miles of the stream belongs to the Hot Creek Ranch, a private resort that offers dry-fly fishing for guests who book its nine cabins. The creek meanders through an open meadow and in the clear water the fish are

easy to spot. Catching them is a different matter—long leaders, sneaky tactics and accurate casting are necessary.

Below the ranch about a mile of fishable stream is open to the public. Then hot water pours into the creek from thermal springs, wiping out the fishing from there until Hot Creek enters the Owens River above Crowley Lake. The hot water keeps the big fish in Hot Creek so they don't migrate to Crowley Lake.

This public access section of Hot Creek is one of the most heavily fished stretches of water in California. It is limited to barbless flies and lures, and is catch-and-release. The walk down to the river from two small parking areas on the dirt road that parallels Hot Creek is fairly steep, but it is only a hundred yards long. The stream itself maintains the same meadow style as on the ranch upstream.

The public access section does not have the same dry-fly restriction as on the ranch and early in the season nymphs are particularly effective.

Both mayflies and caddis are plentiful and nymphs that imitate them such as Hare's Ears, Pheasant Tails, or the AP series in olive, cream or black in about a size 12 are popular. Use of bead-heads can help get the nymphs down faster. There are even a few patterns developed in the area, such as the Burlap Caddis and the Chamois Nymph.

For dries, use any of the classic *Baetis* mayfly imitations such as blue or olive duns. For caddis, try both dark and light imitations up to size 16.

Hot Creek's big fish call for big action, so an excellent technique is to cast good-sized streamers, say a size 6 or 8, into

An Owens River brown—a small one for this river.

openings in the weed beds and strip them back. Favorites are Clouser Minnows, Woolly Buggers and Matukas in dark colors.

Speaking of weed beds, anybody who has fished Hot Creek from about the middle of July on knows all about them. They build up to such an extent that the lanes between them are only a matter of inches and working those lanes is extremely difficult. It also is extremely productive because the trout use the weeds for protection and dart out to take bugs drifting through the water.

Crowley Lake

Fishing Crowley is a must for every California angling enthusiast. Although it is a planted lake the rate of growth is so fast that seven-inchers dumped in May will be 15 inches in October. And it is so big that many of the trout live for years to become five or more pounds.

Although Crowley boasts mayflies and caddis as part of its food chain, midges and perch minnows play the major role. At

and flies, with a two-trout limit of 18 inches or bigger.

Although many fly-line anglers don't fish Crowley until the trophy season, locals say this is a mistake. Float-tubers need to be careful with so many boats on the water but working the area where the Owens River enters Crowley at its northern end can be excellent fishing. It helps that this area is shallow enough so that most boaters stay away.

For many lure and bait anglers opening day on Crowley Lake is a tradition and it is so jammed that you sometimes feel you could walk across it by stepping from boat to boat. By the time the weather heats up most of the boaters have gone to cooler climes.

But Steve Kennedy, who owns The Trout Fitter in Mammoth Lakes, says fishing still is good. "You need to fish the first two hours of day and the last two—these are the times when the fish are feeding in the weed beds." Kennedy adds that although the special restriction season begins August 1, the best fishing is from about mid-September.

certain times of the year, fishing the weed growth along the banks where big trout are feeding on perch minnows, can be exhilarating. Although best fished from a float tube, anglers also can work from the bank.

Crowley has two distinct seasons—until the end of July, when regulations are open, and from August 1 until October 31, which is the trophy season and regulations limit anglers to barbless lures

If you want a break from trout fishing, in May and June the Sacramento perch come into the shallows to spawn. Fishing for them can be fun, not to mention the opportunity to catch a fine eating fish. By August, the perch fry are big enough to imitate with lures and flies and that's when fishing for the big trout that chase them into the bankside weed beds becomes exciting. But since they are in shallow water the trout are spooky, so long, accurate casts are necessary to avoid putting them down.

Float tubes are the favored way to fish. Get out beyond the weed beds and cast in to them. Often anglers can spot working fish, which sometimes seem to be in small schools.

The trout smash these perch fry imitations so heavy leaders are called for—sometimes up to 1X.

Access

The best road to both the western and eastern banks of Crowley is Benton Crossing Road, which turns east off Highway 395 just south of the Mammoth/June Lake Airport. Both the second and third roads turning off to the right lead to the lake. (The first turnoff at the Green Church does not go to Crowley). The second turnoff, at Whitmore Hot Springs, forks after a little more than half a mile. If you stay left from there on you'll end up at the Green Banks section of Crowley Lake, which is good fishing all year around.

Other turnoffs along that road all lead to the lake, but if you keep to the right forks you'll find yourself at Sandy Point.

The third turnoff is just beyond a cattle guard a bit over three miles from Highway 395. It becomes a honeycomb of roads as it approaches Crowley, with the southernmost ending at Green Banks and the northernmost at the West Flats.

To reach the eastern side of the lake, continue along Benton Crossing Road until it crosses the Owens River then turn right .7 of a mile from the bridge. This dirt road goes to the Owens and then splits. Right leads to the upper Owens, left follows the lake shore to East Flats, Weed Point and Leighton Springs. Alligator Point, one of the best fishing areas on Crowley, is about a mile south of where the road ends.

The western side of the southern end of Crowley can be reached by following Highway 395 south until a clearly marked turnoff leads to several bays. This is a boat-launch area and has camping facilities.

To get to the eastern side of southern Crowley, continue a bit further south on Highway 395 and then take the road to Toms Place, which crosses Crowley at the dam. A dirt road where 4-wheel-drive is advisable turns off to the left and offers a number of access points. The Toms Place road also allows access to the Owens River Gorge below the dam.

Lower Owens River

This is a river in the making, already offering good fishing that promises to get even better.

A prime fishery many decades ago, the upper section of the 19-mile Owens River Gorge was reduced to a trickle of water when the Los Angeles Department of Water and Power dammed Crowley Lake and used its water to produce power for the southland. The Owens from the dam down to what is known as the Upper Gorge Power Plant, a distance of about nine miles, remained a viable small-trout stream, fed with water from springs and seepage from Crowley Lake.

The lower 10 miles of the river disappeared—there was no water at all and what once had provided fine fishing became a dusty streambed.

In 1991 a penstock that carried water from the Upper Gorge Power Plant to the turbines broke, spilling water into the desert. The county threatened legal action to get the spilling water diverted into what had been the river, bringing the Los Angeles Department of Water and Power to the negotiating table. The result was an agreement to provide a steady flow of water into the old Owens riverbed, a flow that started at 16 cubic feet per second and is being increased yearly until it is 106 cfs.

With water flowing through the lower gorge again, fishing was restored from the Upper Gorge Plant to Pleasant Valley Reservoir. Plants again began to grow and the caddis, mayflies and other aquatic insects quickly took up residence. The state Department of Fish and Game helped things along by planting wild browns, starting a self-sustaining population that is quickly bringing the river back to at least part of its former glory.

That's the good news. The bad news is that it's a tough place to get to, with rough terrain, broiling summer weather and an occasional rattlesnake to keep anglers company. There's no road that actually leads to the river at the bottom of the 700-foot-deep gorge. The best bet for adventurous anglers is to take the Gorge Road from Highway 395 and park where there is a path or likely area to get to this re-watered 10-mile section of the river.

For easier going, walk in along the two paved roads that lead to the Upper Gorge Power Plant and the Middle Gorge Power Plant and then work your way down to the water. An alternative is to drive in along a dirt road to the Control Gorge Power Plant above Pleasant Valley Reservoir.

Be smart about this: Fish someplace else unless you're in reasonable physical shape, prepared to do some tough scrambling, and are willing to be on a first-name basis with rattlesnakes.

The upper gorge can be reached via the road to Tom's Place that turns off from Highway 395. There are a few spots to park near the river but better fishing can be found by walking downstream along a dirt road. The trout here are much more wary than in the lower gorge—they've been fished over for years.

The Owens River Gorge is open to fishing all year and there are no special regulations.

Also open to fishing year-round is a stretch of the river below Pleasant Valley Reservoir. From the Pleasant Valley Dam downstream to the footbridge at the campground, anglers must use artificial lures and flies and can keep two trout 12 inches or smaller. From the bridge downstream is a 4.4-mile wild trout section that is strictly catch-and-release. This area is extremely popular but offers excellent fishing.

The favored flies are a variety of caddis, Blue-wing Olives, Light Cahills, leech patterns, Woolly Buggers and streamers. For nymphs, the Bead-head Pheasant Tail is the most popular.

For More Information
The Trout Fitter
Shell Mart Center
Highway 203 and Old Mammoth Rd.
Mammoth Lakes, CA 93546
(760) 924-3676

Kittredge Sports
Highway 203 and Forest Trail
Mammoth Lakes, CA 93546
(760) 934-7566

The Trout Fly
Gateway Center
Mammoth Lakes, CA 93546
(760) 934-2517

Rick's Sports Center
Highway 203 and Center Street
Mammoth Lakes, CA 93546
(760) 934-3416

Chapter Sixteen

Kings River

Jeff Boghosian fishing on the wild trout section of the Kings River near Garnett Dike.

Along about March or early April, when spring has warmed the air and it's time to get back to the mountains, it would be great to toss a line into a rushing stream and pull out a few trout. But the general season is closed until late April and fishing lakes and reservoirs just isn't the same thing.

However, there is salvation! It comes in the form of an excellent trout stream that is open to fishing year-round—the Kings River, tucked into the western slope of the Sierra Nevada in Central California southeast of Fresno.

Fishing pressure on most of this river is never heavy. Southern Californians tend to go to the eastern slope of the Sierra while Northern Californians trek to the many fishing areas around Tahoe or head for the Upper Sacramento, McCloud River or Hat Creek. And the Central Valley folks who do fish the Kings are smart enough not to tell the rest of California how good it is and thereby bring in the crowds.

This lack of pressure is the reason the Department of Fish and Game allows trout fishing all year. It also is the reason they don't stock most of the river, so much of the fishing can be for wild trout. While the fish generally don't match the size of those that populate many of the Sierra eastern slope waterways, there still are some browns and rainbows 20 inches and up, although trout half that size are more in the to-be-expected range.

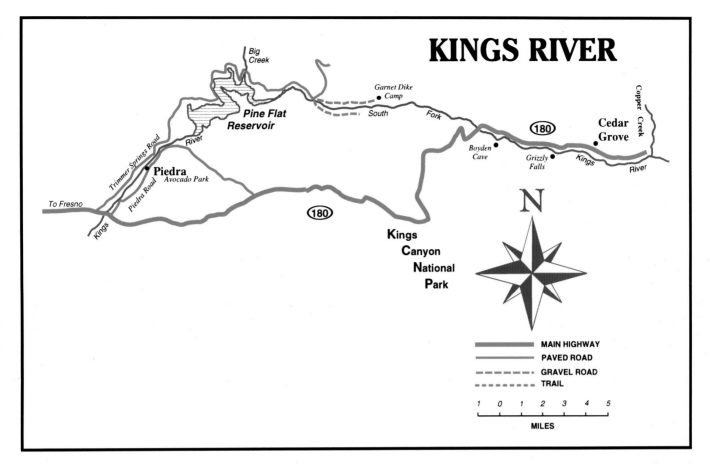

KINGS RIVER

During summer the weather can be hot enough to be miserable. Fall is probably the best and most comfortable fishing but early spring, before the snowmelt turns the river into a torrent, can be productive. While fishing some parts of the Kings is possible all winter, snow precludes fishing the higher sections. Even in the areas that are accessible the water gets cold enough so that trout become lethargic and hard to catch.

The result is sort of a good news/bad news situation—the river is there, it is open all year, it has fish in it and there is little pressure. But fishing it during much of the period when most other streams are closed generally isn't the best time for catching trout.

The Kings River, for fishing purposes, can be broken into three sections—below Pine Flat Reservoir, above Pine Flat Reservoir and near Cedar Grove in the Kings Canyon National Park. Each has a separate character but the sections above and below Pine Flat Reservoir are the only areas that can be reached in winter since they are well below the snow level.

Cedar Grove is at a much higher elevation and the road is not kept open when snow begins to fall, which can be as early as November.

Below Pine Flat Reservoir

The 12-mile stretch of the Kings River from Piedra downstream to Minkler was a fantastic fishery for 14- to 20-inch rainbows several decades ago but a fish kill that wiped out many of the larger fish and then the decision to make it a put-and-take fishery catering to weekend bait-slingers pretty much took care of really big wild trout.

This area now gets so much pressure that there are signs saying it is against the law to drive an auto into the water to wash it. The bank demonstrates a similar urban slum atmosphere and too many of those fishing the area are interested only in taking home as many fish as they can by any means, legal or otherwise.

That's the down side. On the up side there still are some big fish lurking in the riffles and deep pools—just not as many of them.

Except for the area bordered by orange groves and farms, it is easy to access, with two public parks on the river. There are roads on either side of the Kings, Trimmer Springs Road on the north and Piedra Road on the south. They both lead to the little town of Piedra where a bridge crosses the Kings and where most of the public fishing ends since the river then moves onto private property.

The easy access also means this is where fishing pressure is the heaviest, particularly on weekends. Most of the pressure, however, is from anglers who toss bait into the river and wait for something to happen. Aggressive fly anglers or spin fishermen still can take large trout in areas where they can get away from other anglers and put their lures into likely water.

A favorite area, particularly for fly fishers, is behind Avocado Park, which is on the southern bank a couple of miles downstream from the Piedra bridge. One feature of the park is a stocked pond where fishing pressure is heavy. But the Kings flows behind the pond only a hundred feet away and a dirt road leads from either end of the park to the river and the back side of the pond.

At the eastern end of the park where the dirt road joins the river is a large slick that during evening hatches can be dimpled with rising trout. Whether it can be waded depends on how high the water release flow is from Pine Flat Reservoir.

This holds true for the entire stretch so check carefully before attempting to wade, particularly as summer wears on and more water is moving through the river to irrigate downstream farms and orchards.

Caddis are the main hatch and the Kings River Caddis, particularly the parachute version, is effective in sizes 12 through 16.

In winter months the caddis hatch slows but there is almost

always a heavy midge hatch that calls for flies in the 20 to 24 size range. It's tough going but an occasional lunker that has escaped Power Bait and worms can be the prize.

A popular section for locals is just below Piedra bridge, where the river moves quickly around and over boulders that make great holding areas for fish. If you're looking for dinner, this is a place to go, with plenty of stocked rainbows plus some holdovers in the 18-inch range.

Above Pine Flat Reservoir

From Piedra bridge, Trimmer Springs Road leaves the river and winds up to and alongside Pine Flat Reservoir. It is a 25-mile drive around the many arms of the reservoir to reach the Kings River as it enters the lake. One of the arms is Big Creek, which also can be fished upstream from where the road crosses, or downstream when the reservoir is down in low-water years.

The best area to fish the Kings is upstream from where Trimmer Road crosses the river for the second time—a one-lane bridge called the Bailey Bridge. The paved road doubles back and goes into the mountains, but dirt roads on either side of the river allow easy access for fishing and camping. The road on the northern side of the Kings, the far side of the bridge coming from Pine Flat Reservoir, dead-ends after seven miles at Garnet Dike (or Dyke) Campground, where there are toilets, water and camp sites.

Garnet Dike upstream became a wild trout area in 1991 and is favored by fly-line anglers, although the Kings from Garnet Dike downstream to the reservoir hasn't been stocked for decades and is just about as good fishing. The road ends at Garnet Dike but the hike along the riverside trail is not difficult for about three miles. Then it enters a canyon and becomes almost impassable if the water is high.

Garnet Dike is a favorite putting-in spot for spring and early summer rafters, who in high-water years make this stretch of the river a busy spot during the day and can be disruptive to anglers. However, by late afternoon when feeding activity generally picks up the rafters normally are off the river.

The dirt road that follows the southern side of the Kings has several undeveloped camping areas and offers easy river access.

The fishing is the same from either side—riffles, holes and long tailouts. There used to be a lot of big fish in the river here but although trout remain plentiful they are more in the 10- to 14-inch range. This is a spot for the serious angler, particularly for the fly fisher who likes to work nymphs or streamers.

Above Pine Flat can be excellent fishing in early spring before the regular season opens.

A few campers are around on nice weekends and it is almost deserted on weekdays.

About the time the season opens, the snowmelt makes the river too high and too cold for good fishing, although fishing picks up again in the summer. The only drawback during summer is that temperatures are hot enough to be uncomfortable.

From Garnet Dike Camp, the Kings is not accessible by road until it picks up Highway 180 near Boyden Cave in the Sequoia National Forest nearly 10 miles upstream.

Upper Kings River

Larry Goates, manager of Buz's Fly Shop in Visalia, says that the upper Kings River in Kings Canyon National Park "is the best fishery on the west side of the Sierra." Goates, a native of Visalia who has guided in the area for years, says the river is incredibly prolific. "What the river lacks in sizable fish it makes up in quantity," he says, adding that "it is hard not to catch fish here."

From where Highway 180 drops into the canyon and picks up

the river at Boyden Cave to where it dead-ends at Copper Creek is about 17 miles, with Cedar Grove Village at mid-point. From Boyden Cave to Cedar Grove the river rushes through the canyon, providing only fast-water fishing that makes it tough for fly anglers until late in the summer when the water level drops. However, from Cedar Grove to Copper Creek the river slows considerably, offering much easier fishing.

Copper Creek is a major trailhead with long-term parking for hikers headed into the backcountry. It also is an excellent jumping-off spot for anglers to work upstream to where Bubb's Creek enters the Kings, an easy two-mile hike.

Goates recommends fishing from Cedar Grove upstream early in the summer as soon as the runoff is low enough to allow wading. There is no stocking on the Kings—it is a wild trout area —which means that bait fishing can be less productive than with planted areas.

A two-trout limit also discourages fishing for many anglers. As a result, even in the area near the Cedar Grove campgrounds fly anglers can find excellent action early in the summer, particularly with smaller fish.

For the record, like the lower Kings River this section is open to fishing year-round but the road is not kept open in the winter when snowfall begins.

Goates says that from Cedar Grove upstream the river "yields extremely well to the fly but not to the spin fisherman. This is one of the worst spin-fishing rivers because it is shallow and wide— the average depth is probably around two or three feet." For bait anglers he recommends the Grizzly Falls area about three miles downstream from Cedar Grove.

As with many rivers, this section of the Kings offers different fishing possibilities at different times of the year.

After fishing the Cedar Grove to Bubb's Creek area during the early summer, Goates says, "In August I start going downstream and fish along the road. It's rougher down there, not meadowy as it is upstream. But from Grizzly Falls to Boyden Cave the fish get bigger, averaging 10 inches and getting up to 15 or 20 inches. Most of the big fish are browns but two of the biggest I know that have been caught were rainbows."

Goates says that, "hatches on the Kings are not prolific. Caddis hatches are sporadic throughout the year, large salmonflies happen in late May and June. In June there are some larger mayfly species and during that period fishing can be non-stop. I've hooked 30 or 40 fish in two hours during an evening—one every cast."

On October 1 the store at Cedar Grove closes and the visitor level drops drastically. It's then, Goates says, that the area offers the best fishing, even though it is surrounded by campgrounds. It's that area he fishes until snow closes the road.

"I use attractor patterns, with a preference for the Western Coachman. It can be swung wet style and take fish or be greased and fished dry. There are some times of year when you get small, cream mayflies coming off and a Royal Wulff isn't going to catch as many as a size 16 Light Cahill. But for the most part throughout the year if you have something like an Elk Hair Caddis or Coachman or Wulff it's fine."

He recommends size 10 through 16—"I've never needed to use anything smaller than a size 16 on this river."

For More Information

Buz's Fly Shop
400 N. Johnson
Visalia, CA 93291
(209) 734-1151

Range of Light Fly Fishing Outfitters
2020 W. Whitendale
Visalia, CA 93277
(209) 635-1500

Jeff Boghosian, guide
(209) 229-5640

Jace Deese takes a nap during the midle of the day on the Upper Sacramento River.

CALIFORNIA BLUE-RIBBON TROUT STREAMS

LEARN MORE ABOUT FLY FISHING AND FLY TYING WITH THESE BOOKS

If you are unable to find the books shown below at your local book store
or fly shop you can order direct from the publisher below.

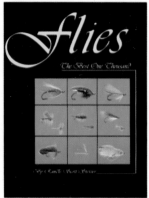

Flies: The Best One Thousand
Randy Stetzer
$24.95

Fly Tying Made Clear and Simple
Skip Morris
$19.95 (HB: $29.95)

The Art of Tying the Dry Fly
Skip Morris
$29.95 (HB:$39.95)

Curtis Creek Manifesto
Sheridan Anderson
$7.95

American Fly Tying Manual
Dave Hughes
$9.95

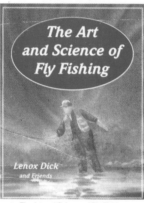

The Art and Science of Fly Fishing
Lenox Dick
$19.95

Western Hatches
Dave Hughes, Rick Hafele
$24.95

Lake Fishing with a Fly
Ron Cordes, Randall Kaufmann
$26.95

Advanced Fly Fishing for Steelhead
Deke Meyer
$24.95

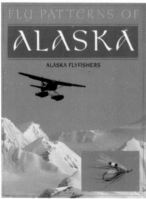

Fly Patterns of Alaska
Alaska Flyfishers
$19.95

Fly Tying & Fishing for Panfish and Bass
Tom Keith
$19.95

Float Tube Fly Fishing
Deke Meyer
$11.95

VISA, MASTERCARD or AMERICAN EXPRESS ORDERS CALL TOLL FREE: 1-800-541-9498
(9-5 Pacific Standard Time)

Or Send Check or money order to:

Frank Amato Publications
Box 82112
Portland, Oregon 97282

(Please add $3.00 for shipping and handling)